DATE DUE			
APR 2 4 1992			
MAY 1 4 1992			
MAY 1 1 1993			
MAY 5 1994			
MAR 8 - 1996			
MAR 2 7 1996			
MAR 1 8 2000			
AUG 3 0 2007			
APR 2 7 2011			
FEB 1 0 2015			

the
alchemy
of
awareness

the
alchemy
of
awareness

lorraine
sinkler

Harper & Row, Publishers
New York, Hagerstown, San Francisco, London

Designed by Janice Stern   79 80 81 10 9 8 7 6 5 4 3

Library of Congress Cataloging in Publication Data

Sinkler, Lorraine.
   The alchemy of awareness.

   1. Spiritual life. I. Title.
BL624.S58   1977   248'.4   76–62957
ISBN 0–06–067387–7

CONTENTS

Part Two: Building the Temple

PREFACE

When a person picks up a book to read, it is usually for some purpose: to while away an empty hour, for pleasure, for information, to find the answer to some problem, to fill an emptiness within, or to seek to understand the meaning of life. What is your purpose in reading this book? What are you seeking? Perhaps you will find something in it to hold your interest during that empty hour, or it may lead you to a greater understanding of the nature of your being.

In July of 1959, at the request of my teacher Joel Goldsmith, I flew to Hawaii to manage his 1959 Hawaiian Village Closed Class. Being there also provided an opportunity for me to confer with Joel about material to be used in projected new books and to show him the corrected galley proofs of his forthcoming book *The Art of Spiritual Healing*. As he sat in the spacious living room at Halekou Place one Sunday afternoon reading the proofs, I sat across the room working on the manuscript for his next book. Suddenly Joel looked up from his reading and asked, "Why don't you write a book of your own?"

I was stunned by that question. I had never thought of doing anything but assembling material from Joel's tape recordings, organizing it into books, and eventually writing his biography. Finally I recovered sufficiently to answer, "Because I wouldn't know where you left off, and I began." That has been my quandary all these years and even more so now, after having edited and prepared for publication twenty-four of Joel's books. That is why I have never attempted to write anything of my own other than *The Spiritual Journey of Joel S. Goldsmith.*

Because of much urging from students of The Infinite Way, I have set forth in *The Alchemy of Awareness* a distillation of my own experiences with the principles Joel taught me, during my long years of association with him. If much of Joel has crept into it, the reason is that I still do not know where Joel leaves off and I begin. But here it is, and I am sure that Joel is happy.

I have tried to show, in ways as specific and concrete as possible, how the principles of The Infinite Way can be applied to daily life and why the spiritual path can be a practical and intelligent way of life. This book will be meaningful to you, however, only if you live these principles, so that through an inner revelation of spiritual reality and spiritual identity the broader purpose of life can be fulfilled in you. The principles must be practiced. Are you willing to work with them?

L.S.

Palm Beach, Florida

ACKNOWLEDGMENTS

Many persons have played a significant role in the unfoldment of *The Alchemy of Awareness*. To these I give my heartfelt gratitude:

Joel S. Goldsmith, my teacher, whose matchless instruction, unfailing encouragement, and spiritual support inspired and led me step by step to ever greater awareness;

Infinite Way students, hundreds of them, who have studied with me individually and in classes and who, through their penetrating questions, have compelled me to bring to a focus the application of the principles of The Infinite Way;

Shirley A. Woods, whose spirit of generosity and cooperation has been expressed in typing innumerable rough drafts of the manuscript;

Margaret Wacker Davis, who, with love and dedication for more than twenty years, has expertly typed the final manuscripts of all but six of Joel Goldsmith's books as well as my own;

Gwen Freer Sharer, who lovingly shared her expertise by making suggestions which were invaluable in the preparation of the book;

Valborg Sinkler Crossland, my beloved sister, without whose expert help, understanding, and encouragement this book could never have been written. Of our relationship Joel Goldsmith said, "You and Valborg are so much one that you are really one person with two heads and four hands."

PART ONE

FOUNDATION STONES

1

An Even Balance

Let me be weighed in an even balance, that
God may know mine integrity.

Job 31:6

The basic fears of mankind inherent in human consciousness have never been satisfactorily resolved. Consequently fear is the climate in which most persons live today. Even when they do achieve a measure of safety, love, understanding, wholeness, completeness, peace, or joy, there is always the fear of losing it, so a life lived without fear, secure in the essential goodness of life, eludes most persons. Is that not because they are looking in the wrong place, looking for their good outside themselves and putting their faith and trust in some particular thing or person? And does not dependence on human beings and material possessions turn out to be a false reliance which usually fails in the end? As long as persons rely on what is visible, on what they can see, touch, and handle, their every effort is directed toward drawing what they think is their good to themselves.

Since the visible exists only in limited amounts, it naturally follows that what is already in existence must either be divided among the people of the world or be subtracted from one person to give to another. The fear thus generated results in strife not only on a personal level but on an international scale, bringing with it frustration, disappointment, unhappiness, and an increase in mental illness.

Much research has been done in an attempt to determine the overriding cause of nervous disorders. Why not reverse that?

3

Should not psychiatrists and social scientists be carrying on more research as to why it is possible for some persons to go through traumatic experiences, face the most difficult problems, endure the greatest catastrophes, and yet emerge untouched? Could it be that those who are able to weather devastating experiences and come through them unscathed have an enduring sense of values?

Enduring values can never be found in any material thing or even in a person, because both things and persons have a way of disappearing or eluding us. Enduring values can be found only in that which goes beyond the visible, that which can never be known with the senses and yet is more real and tangible than the material world, that from which a person can never be separated because it is an integral part of his being.

Throughout the centuries there have been a few who have sought satisfaction and fulfillment, not in the outer world, but in an entirely different direction. In their seeking they have started on a long journey which will take them to the heights of consciousness.

The first turning away from the frustrations of life nearly always comes with the realization that there must be something better than the everyday struggle and strife. This realization is an awakening to the Presence within, a barely perceptible crack in the hard crust of humanhood. It is like a little candle shining faintly in the dark world of human consciousness with its separate life to be preserved and with a self that fears, struggles, and battles. But even with that faint glimmer of light, attention for the most part stays riveted on the things of the world. Thus when the satisfactions of life begin to come, they are soon consumed and wither because they are still dependent on the transient trappings and values of the visible world.

Maintaining a Spiritual Balance

Despite the almost insuperable barriers to the search for that which is beyond the visible, the seeker, led on by the expectation that there must be something permanent, enduring, and true, tries to find a way to realize what at first may have seemed but a vain hope. The way is called by many names and has many labels, but essentially it is a path that leads through the maze of conflicting theories and beliefs right to the heart of reality.

So difficult is the Path to travel that it has been called "the razor's edge." We can think of that Path as a narrow road leading up to the summit of a towering mountain with a deep chasm on one side, stretching far below like a bottomless pit, and on the other side a vortex of water. To travel that perilous road, the seeker must not look at the dangers lurking below but must keep his attention fixed firmly on the summit to be reached.

Following the Path may also bring to mind the familiar picture of a tightrope walker, navigating the distance from one point to another on a rope stretched so high above the ground that a single misstep could mean disaster. The tightrope walker, however, keeps his eyes fastened upon the goal, which to the onlooker seems quite a short distance but which to that performer, as he sets out on his hazardous course, must seem an eternity away. He does not look down at the danger below. He does not count the cost. He keeps his eyes straight ahead and goes steadily forward.

What is it that makes such an achievement possible? We, too, might attempt it, keep our eyes on the goal, and still not succeed. Only one thing makes it possible: perfect balance. If we are going to walk the razor's edge, we will need an even more perfect balance than that required of the tightrope walker or the mountain climber.

The spiritual aspirant must be able to live effectively in the world, meeting his human responsibilities, yet retaining an inner area of consciousness devoted primarily to spiritual attainment and open only to the spiritual impulse. How many times do students on the spiritual path appear to others a little bit odd, crackpots? Perhaps that reputation has been earned because of an inability to maintain the spiritual balance which makes it possible to be in the world, functioning efficiently and effectively, and yet not be of it.

To what extent can we stay in the marketplace, surrounded by the competition, struggle, strife, and jealousy characteristic of the business or professional world, and yet maintain an awareness of a Power, a Presence, and a Realm unknown to the materialistic world-consciousness? It takes spiritual balance, the ability not to veer to one side or the other but always to blend the outer and the inner in one harmonious whole. To do this our whole day cannot be given over to worldly pursuits, but neither should it be given over entirely to meditation. True, we meditate many times a day to maintain an awareness of the Presence, but then we must go out and live this awareness by meeting the daily challenges and opportunities the world provides. It is possible to be in the world and yet live apart from it if we understand spiritual principles which help to maintain that necessary balance.

The mystical way is one of intense inner stillness in the midst of incredible outer activity. Certainly no one will deny that Christ Jesus was a great mystic. Yet he went out into the bypaths of the world, up and down the countryside, healing the sick, comforting those who mourned, raising the dead, and supplying those in need. Jesus was a man of action, even though unattached to the world.

To attain the awareness which transforms consciousness calls for a nonattachment to the things and persons of the world. If we were to be completely nonattached, however, we would float in a kind of vacuum with no base on which to rest. Some attachment is necessary, and it must be to something real and eternal. This can be found only in the Spirit within, which becomes our anchor. Then, as a deeper awareness of that Spirit, which is all-presence, all-power, and all-love, increases so that we know that we are inseparable and indivisible from It, we become less and less attached to the ephemeral, constantly shifting and changing pictures of the human world. Eventually we will be able to see right through them to the reality which lies beyond. This is the balance of the spiritual path.

It is folly for anyone to attempt to live beyond his attained state of consciousness. We would all like to reach a state of consciousness which would enable us to prove our spirituality by walking on the water, but we recognize that we have not attained the consciousness of a Christ Jesus. So we take a boat. Each one on the Path must have enough perception and wisdom to assess his degree of developed consciousness and not let the ego push him into trying to "walk on the water" before he is ready.

There is an eternal balance in the universe: the earth moves in its orbit according to fixed law; the planets maintain a right relationship one to another; all the activities of nature follow a law of divine order except where man has stepped in and upset the balance of nature by polluting the air and water. The balance of the planets thus far has not been upset. Perhaps that is because man did not think he was quite capable of trying to change that, even though his conceit might surely tempt him.

Is not every difficulty we face, in a sense, a matter of imbalance? If we begin our journey on the Path by remembering the importance of spiritual balance, keeping our perspective with the vision always before us, with our heads in the clouds and our feet on the ground, we may be able to walk the razor's edge and attain the goal.

Toward Illumination

It takes perseverance. Anyone who aspires to walk the straight and narrow path to illumination must have the courage to continue in the face of all obstacles. Paul said, "I press toward the mark of the prize for the high calling of God in Christ Jesus." Let us also press forward, step by step, to gain that prize, for it is well worth every effort. It is reported that Socrates once told a traveler who asked him how to reach Mount Olympus, "Make every step you take go in the right direction." As we make every step we take lead us toward that awareness which will transform our entire experience, we draw closer to the spiritual goal. We must not be like Pliable and Obstinate in *Pilgrim's Progress* who gave up the journey to the Celestial City because they ran into a bog that dragged them down.

Yes, not only is effort required and persistence in that effort, but no one can tread the razor's edge without the requisite spiritual balance. As we contemplate the divine Wisdom, It* reveals whatever is necessary for us to do and gives us the strength and courage to press on. Then we walk the way with confidence and assurance, knowing that we do not walk alone, but That within us goes before us, ever leading us forward to peace and fulfillment. "This is the way, walk ye in it."

This straight and narrow path takes us right to the Center of our being. When we touch that Center, it is as if a light had been turned on inside of us. As awareness increases, that very dim light grows and expands until one day the whole universe is encompassed by the light in which we are now living. Thus the straight and narrow path becomes a broad highway.

It is a glorious way but nonetheless difficult, because when the light shines on all the rubbish lodged in our consciousness that rubbish must be cleared out. If, for example, we were to go into a room in which there was no light, the room might be filled with all kinds of old papers, dust, dirt, and broken-down furniture which we could not see in the darkness. But when even a flickering candle is lighted in that room, we see the cobwebs and the dirt and begin the process of cleaning it out.

This is much like what happens on the road to illumination. The light shines in the dark places of consciousness, and those dark places have to be cleared away. Just as it takes work and effort to clean up a dirty room, it takes ten thousandfold more effort to clean out a mind that has been cluttered with all kinds of beliefs —beliefs to which the world remains in bondage.

In fact, everyone is living under a measure of bondage. With

*"He" and "It," "Himself" and "Itself," and "Me" and "My," when capitalized, refer to God.

some it is a bondage to lack and limitation with no sense of inner security. Others with much of the world's goods are still in bondage to their pocketbooks and persist in holding on to their possessions. Still others live in bondage to a body or to the constricted and limited life that fear engenders.

The Choice

Those who have set their feet upon the spiritual path, however, have embarked upon the road to the only real freedom there is, a freedom not dependent on exterior forms or conditions. They have caught a glimpse of the Center within and live out from that instead of living on something external to themselves. Gradually they relinquish the idea that any situation or any person has power to act upon them either for good or for evil. That is a startling idea. Who has not thought that his good came from some person, or that the evil he was experiencing came because someone had directed evil toward him or had withheld something he felt was his?

Even a small measure of awareness reveals that we are not the victims of persons or circumstances. If we want to enjoy more peace and harmony, a quietness, a confidence, and an assurance, however, we must nurture a growing awareness of That within which is more powerful than anything or any set of things in the world. To do this calls for an about-face because heretofore our attention has been directed toward getting, achieving, and obtaining.

We have a choice. We can climb to the top of the mountain, where the vision is clearer, by that steep, straight road that takes us directly there, or we can meander around for another dozen lifetimes. Someday we will arrive, but the swiftness or speed of our journey will be determined by our dedication and consecration.

Those who engage in mountain climbing as a sport are willing to face every hazard along the way as a challenge, not as something to dread but as a hurdle to be surmounted. As we scale the mountain, let us look upon every experience that comes to us as one of those hurdles which we leap over to go on beyond. A challenge is an opportunity. For us it is an opportunity to surrender every human dependence and to rely entirely upon the Withinness, thereby losing the human sense of life in the Divine.

Total surrender does not mean resignation. Resigning oneself to enduring endless problems is a negative approach. Surrender is a giving up of the negative so that the perfect will of God may be revealed and expressed. It is hard and painful only because most of us cling to the personal sense of self and resist surrendering it.

A knowledge and workable understanding of the principles of construction are necessary for an engineer planning and supervising the building of a bridge or a highway, and for an architect drafting the plans for a building. So, too, for us to rise to the heights of spiritual awareness, a thorough working knowledge of the principles of spiritual living and healing is required. We all like to float on Cloud Nine, or better yet, on Cloud Ninety-nine, and rest there. But a cloud is not a very solid resting place. If we were flying in a jet plane above a beautiful white cloud, and if the engines failed, we would not take much comfort in the cloud because it could not possibly support a falling plane. So if those moments of heightened awareness come to one who is truly seeking but who has no background of specific principles, he may find himself tumbling down, down, down, right into the valley, where he has to begin the ascent all over again.

But when we have certain principles as a foundation, they serve as a basis from which we can climb to the very heights of consciousness. If we have no foundation on which to rest, it is very difficult to attain and maintain that higher consciousness which can see beyond the immediate situation or problem.

To climb the mount of spiritual awareness by an uncharted path can be a very difficult, hazardous, and tortuous job. But when the way is well marked by principles discovered by those who have gone before, many of the hazards and difficulties are removed or lessened, though the way may still offer its full measure of challenges.

The Spirit pushes and pulls us toward Itself until one day, when we are done with all our toys and games, weary of the struggle, the toil, and the unfruitful labor, we wonder if there is not something greater than ourselves. It is in that moment that we are called to a spiritual way of life.

2

There Was Silence in Heaven

There was silence in heaven about the space
of half an hour.

Revelation 8:1

Some years ago on an especially rough crossing from Australia to Hawaii, the waves dashed against the sides of our ship, tossing it hither and yon so that it seemed about as stable as a cork in a seething cauldron. As I watched the foaming sea, it came to me that if it were possible to go far below the surface of the water, deep down into the ocean, there would be no turbulence, just a rhythmic movement characterized by quietness and serenity.

When we live on externals we are much like that ship, buffeted about by every wind that blows. Our whole life is at the beck and call of human laws and material powers, with turmoil, dissatisfaction, grief, and frustration the end product. Not so if we learn to live out from Consciousness and go deep within to our Center where there is an eternal peace untouched by external effects, a peace always available and just awaiting recognition.

For most of us, the problem is learning how to reach this Center which will bring us such a peace. One of the most effective ways is through the practice of meditation, which enables us to take a high dive off the springboard of this world into the ocean of Spirit, swimming out beyond the horizon, letting the waters of Spirit carry us ever deeper within, then surfacing in a state of perfect relaxation, floating free from all tension, and resting in our own divine Beingness. There is neither strain nor mental effort as long as It carries us.

Right now you and I are one with the Father, who knows our every need. We say that, and then in the next breath tell the Father what things we need, forgetting that it is the Father's good pleasure to give us, not things, but the fullness of life. But what does fullness of life mean? Does it mean that more of the material things of this world will be ours? Does it mean having x number of dollars or so many acres of land? No, God knows nothing about the things of the world, a truth of which many persons are unaware.

Not long ago I received a letter from a woman who asked me to meditate and go to God to get her a new refrigerator and a new air conditioner. My answer was that if she wanted things, she should write to Santa Claus, and I explained that God is not Santa Claus.

A serious student of meditation could well ask himself: What is the purpose of meditation? Am I meditating because I hope it will do something for me, that is, bring me more of the world's good: increased supply, a better position, better relationships, a healthier body? Contrary to a common misconception, meditation cannot be used to try by sheer mental effort to force God to do our will and to bring us what we want. Rather, it is a way of attaining a sufficient degree of silence so that the Spirit within can impart Itself to us. The quickest way to attain that silence is to give up every desire and let the Spirit determine what is necessary so that It may be fulfilled as us.

Surrender

To succeed in meditation there must be a surrender of all hopes, desires, fears, and concepts, a "not my will, but thine be done." That is hard to do because we forget or do not realize that the divine will can be measured only in terms of infinity, wholeness, perfection, a peace that is beyond understanding, and a joy no man can take from us. Understanding that to be the divine will, it is less difficult to surrender to the will of God and to lose every human desire. If we ask for some *thing* in meditation, we may get it and live to regret it. But when we have God's grace and God's love there will never be any regrets, because that infinite Wisdom knows what is necessary for spiritual fulfillment, and that Wisdom then translates Itself into whatever is needed. But we do not seek the translation: we seek the Source.

I surrender every hope, for there is nothing for which I need to hope. I need only to awaken to the fulfillment that now is. No good can come to me, because all good is now established in my individual consciousness, which is the infinite divine Consciousness.

I give up all fear. What can I fear in the presence of Love, in the presence of Life beginningless and endless? Fear has no power over me, for God has not given me the spirit of fear, but of love and of a sound mind.

I surrender my mind, for it never was my mind but an instrument to mirror forth the divine activity. My mind is a transparency through which the isness of God can be revealed. Nothing I can ever do will make God more than God is, and nothing I can do will make God less than God is. I rest in is. God is now being, and I am being.

I surrender my body to the divine government that it may be what it was intended to be: a temple to show forth God's glory, God's perfection, God's wholeness. Under that divine government neither laws of matter nor laws of mind operate. Grace is in operation and is governing my body, which is formed of spiritual substance.

I surrender all my possessions, everything I thought I owned. They never were mine. "The earth is the Lord's, and the fulness thereof." That which is belongs to the Father, and the Father has given His all to me for His purpose, not mine. I am but the custodian, the distributing center, through which the good of God pours forth.

I surrender every desire, even the desire to help anyone. I let the grace of God permeate my mind and body, permeate and fill the

consciousness I am, so that everyone who is a part of this conscious-
ness may feel that Grace. I do not direct It, nor do I have any desire
as to where It should go. I sit here as an instrument through which
Grace is flowing, knowing that It is divine intelligence, the all-
knowing.

I consciously surrender this personal sense of Self. I lay it on the
altar that the little I may grow less and less, so that the I that I
am may increase. I, with all my hopes and fears and desires, must
decrease that I may increase. *

When we have surrendered to the divine will and have no desire, no hope, and no fear, the mind becomes still. That does not mean that the mind is a blank. There is an activity going on, not the activity of our hopes, fears, dreads, or desires, but the activity of the Spirit within which is doing the thinking, no longer our thoughts, but Its thoughts.

Meditation should always be undertaken with an attitude of unknowing. As long as we believe that we know any truth or even know how to meditate, the door to new unfoldments is closed, whereas when we are willing to sit in a state of complete unknowingness, the door is ever open for greater unfoldment. Living in a state of constant expectancy, watching to see what God is unfolding for us every moment of the day, we become receptive to the divine impulse.

No special words are needed to stand in the presence of God. The intents of the heart and the motive in prayer and meditation are what count. If that motive is pure and single-minded sometimes God will reveal Itself, even in a moment when we have no awareness of having made any kind of a conscious contact, or in a moment of not thinking when there is a complete silencing of human planning, thought, and will.

If a certain combination of words were necessary, that would

*The italicized portions of this book are meditations that came to the author in moments of heightened awareness.

make God dependent upon an effect. And what kind of a God would that be? Words are unimportant in approaching God. Instead let us go to God with the same attitude one child had as she sat almost hidden in the midst of a field of waving wheat. When her grandfather went looking for her, from a distance he heard her going through the entire alphabet, softly saying, "A, B, C, D, E . . .".

Curious, her grandfather asked, "Carol, what are you doing?"

"I'm praying, Grandpa. But I don't know the right words, so I am saying all the letters and letting God put them together."

Persistence, Patience, and Practice Essential

Some of us may have to meditate for a long time before anything comes. There may be very little feeling or response, or none whatsoever. Life goes along in much the same pattern, like an old record repeating itself. There seems to be a sameness, a dullness, even a deadness. If we are devoting ourselves to the practice of meditation, however, there comes a time when a tremendous impetus is given to our whole experience, and suddenly we feel a movement in consciousness as if the whole of heaven has opened up, pouring out its wonder and glory into our consciousness. That does not just happen or come about in a hit-or-miss way. It comes because of the faithfulness with which we have persisted in meditation for weeks, months, and possibly years.

If we wish to progress on the Path we must set aside time for meditation, because as human beings our whole attention is usually so focused on the things of the world that it is difficult to turn away from that clamor and become still. Too often, however, some of us strain when we try to meditate, strain and struggle to become relaxed. But if we would begin our meditation with deep humility, recognizing that we of ourselves do not know how to meditate and are not trying to force something to happen, we could settle down into a relaxed state that makes meditation easier. We could not breathe were there not Something in us which is breathing, and certainly we could not meditate were it not for that Something that is doing it. Let our attitude be:

Father, here I am. Of myself I cannot meditate. But I am willing to be an instrument through which You speak the word. You meditate and let me be a witness to Your meditating in me and through me.

Of myself I can do nothing. I do not know how to pray. I do not know how to go into meditation or how to go out of meditation. But You, Father, within me, You know all things. You, Father, can do all things. You meditate in me. I open myself in a receptive state, letting You do the meditating, letting You use me as Your instrument.

If you do this a dozen times a day—and forty would be better —for a minute or thirty seconds, you will become increasingly aware of the Presence and Power within. If your meditation should last for a whole minute, that would indeed be remarkable. Do not watch the clock. Meditate only for a short time, only for as long as your mind is still. When your mind becomes restless, be willing to stop.

A person who meditates is a little like a stone cutter who, in attempting to cut a stone in half, strikes it perhaps as many as ninety-nine times without success. Then on the one hundredth stroke the stone breaks. Did it break at the hundredth stroke or did it break because of the ninety-nine preceding blows?

So it is with meditation. You may not feel a thing, but as you follow through with this practice, you are cultivating the seed within you, watering it, giving it attention and an opportunity to break open its shell. The more you practice letting the Father do the meditating, the easier it becomes to fall into meditation.

Seven years before I met my teacher, Joel Goldsmith, I had begun to meditate. At that time there was no one to guide me, nothing except innumerable recipes for inner attainment I found in many different books. All these books emphasized the importance of posture, and from them I gathered that those who attained meditation usually sat in a cross-legged position on the floor. For weeks I obediently struggled to feel at ease while sitting for ten minutes at a time on the floor with my legs crossed.

During the practice periods the minutes ticked by slowly. Ten minutes seemed an interminable length of time. Never once did I think about God. All I could think about was how my legs hurt. Instead of realizing God, I was conscious only of how miserable I felt, which gave rise to some doubt as to whether the spiritual way of life was meant for a person as undisciplined physically as I. Later I was relieved to discover that The Infinite Way gave little importance to posture as a means of attaining spiritual light. It emphasized only being sufficiently comfortable so that the body is out of mind and attention can be centered on the goal.

With the problem of posture resolved, I abandoned myself wholeheartedly to the adventure awaiting me, an adventure in which life began to take on new luster and joyous expectancy became the order of the day. In fact, this feeling is sometimes almost like being in love, when no sacrifice is too great to be with one's beloved. Motivated by a love for God so great that we are willing to make any effort and any sacrifice to be in His presence and to feel His ever flowing love, meditation becomes more of a joy than an arduous practice engaged in for some selfish purpose.

Listening for an Impartation From Within

Sitting for hours and hours reading about meditation will never make for proficiency in the art. The amount and kind of practice is all-important. For example, in the next twenty-four hours stop frequently, every half hour if possible, to remember: "I already am in the presence of God, the Source of all life. I already am in the presence of fulfillment." Remind yourself: "I live and move and have my being in divine Consciousness." Use anything as a reminder that there is Something within that carries you through every experience, Something that is living Its life as you.

God is forever pouring forth Its wisdom if only we open ourselves to It. It is really that simple and that difficult. Why difficult? Because simple things are always difficult to the human mentality which thinks that unless a thing is hard it is neither worthwhile nor important. So the simple things that might enable a person to make great strides on the Path are often ignored.

God is being: God is always doing and always being. Our purpose in meditation is to become aware of the beingness of God, to receive impartations from the divine Consciousness. Yet it should be remembered that God is not imparting Itself specifically to us. God is always imparting Itself, but unless we are turning within we will be as unaware of Its message as we would be of a television program that we had not tuned our set to receive. It is through meditation that we become aware of God's continuous broadcasting of His love, His goodness, and His infinity, and become a witness to God revealing Himself.

God is always waiting for us right where we are. Never can we be separated from His presence. Never does He desert or forsake us, no matter what we do. Sometimes, however, we forsake God and forget Him because we do not love Him enough. When we love God with all our heart and with all our mind, with a singleness of purpose, and have felt His presence, we can never again be satisfied to be outside of It. If temporarily the world overwhelms us, even then the Presence will not let us go.

Meditation which brings us into conscious contact with our Source can be carried on wherever we are—while working in an office, about our home, or in the midst of a business conference. Wherever we are, we can pause and meditate even with our eyes open. In that pause we are shutting out the world and opening ourselves to the spiritual Presence and Power.

Real meditation or prayer is listening. It is not an attempt to tell God anything. A mother who was trying to convey this idea to a group of children asked, "Have you ever tried to carry on a conversation with someone who interrupted you all the time so that you didn't get a chance to say anything at all?"

"Yeah," one of them responded, "some guys want to talk all the time, but I interrupt them and I just put in my two cents, too, even when they keep on talking."

This was the mother's opportunity. "Well, God is a perfect Gentleman, and He never interrupts. So if you want to go rambling on and on, God will just let you keep talking because He would never interrupt you. But if you want to hear God speak to you, you have to be still and listen, and when you are very quiet, God will tell you what He has to say to you."

That should be our cue to form the habit of turning within with a "Here I am, Father. You do the talking. You speak to me." Then wait a few seconds, not for long, just a few seconds. Those few seconds of waiting are important because in them we have as much as said, "Father, You take over."

In other words, we have declared our humility, and meditation does demand humility. It is the recognition that of our own selves we can do nothing. But it is also the recognition that there is Something within that knows all things, and we are turning to that Something for Its sustenance, support, and wisdom with the attitude: "I have no concept of what You should say to me, Father, of how You should speak, or what You should do for me. I'm just waiting attentively and alertly, listening for what You have to say." If we begin a practice such as this for a minute or for even a few seconds, eventually we find ourselves consciously living in the presence of God.

What the fifteen-year-old son of a friend of mine wrote in his theme "A Letter from God" should be an inspiration to everyone starting out on the path of inner contemplation and listening.

A letter from God is like a letter from just about anyone. It is not something to be afraid of. It is just something containing ideas to think about. You see, God is not an overpowering admonishing Deity to be prostrated before and to whom we continually beg and plead.

If only people could realize this, they might be able to accept what God tells them in His letter and accept it for what it is. God is always busy running down to the post office at all hours of the night and every waking hour, doing nothing but sending out His letters. God is always writing us His letters, and they are as plain and simple as if our best friend were writing us, if you know what has been said before and get the whole message.

All we have to do to write our letter is to close our eyes, remember that He is as close to us as our own breathing and say, "Okay, God, here I am listening to You as You write me. We are corresponding again, and now maybe we will really understand each other."

Is that not the function of meditation or prayer: to open ourselves to the messages God is always sending us? Is it not comforting to know that they are as plain and simple as if our best friend were writing to us? So in our meditation let us feel that we are beginning to correspond with God. We are beginning to get acquainted again. God does not have to get acquainted with us because He already knows all there is to know about us in our spiritual identity as His beloved son in whom there is no fault.

But we do not know our tender, loving Father. We have been trained to believe that this loving Father is an awesome Being, to be approached with fear and trembling. Does any person like to be approached in that way? Perhaps unimportant persons might, but not those who are really accomplishing things. They like to be approached in a simple and direct way, and that is the way we should approach the Presence within. If we wander far afield and forget this Presence, our forgetting makes no difference to It. It keeps right on being a light at the center of our being, a light which is always shining and a voice which is always speaking.

Approach Meditation With a Relaxed Attitude of Joyous Expectancy

Some persons have little success with meditation because they try to meditate for too long a time. The net result is that it becomes a mental strain and they end up with a headache or a backache. They go into meditation with a kind of grim determination. On the contrary, it should be approached as we would a banquet. At a banquet the guests sit down to the table with a sense of expectancy, ready to savor the food that has been prepared and is waiting for them. That is the way it should be with meditation, except that at the banquet of meditation the food God has prepared does not spoil from waiting, nor does it deteriorate in any way.

Why not sit down to the banquet of meditation with joy, expecting that God will be revealed in silence? In this way we may have the Experience, not just a talking about it but a revelation of that which is beyond knowledge but which can be experienced in the silence. In the silence, the Presence reminds us that It will never leave us no matter in what desert of human experience we may be lost. It will make for us a way, and even as we walk through the desert, the desert itself is transformed into a garden. We need never fear that we will not find the way or that we will lose it, because there is within us That which is the way:

I, *the presence of God within you, am the way which leads to fulfillment and to eternal life. Do not seek a way. Do not seek for a sign. Find Me at the center of your being. I will lead you step by step. I will make the rocks along the way stepping stones, and the winding road I will make straight, the road leading straight to the center of life.*

Even if we try we cannot get away from God. We cannot be separated from the *I** that we are, for God is our very own being, so close that the only name for It is *I.* Are we conscious every moment that we are breathing? Is it not only when there is no air to breathe that we find ourselves struggling for it? Why then struggle to reach God?

When I look out my window at the ocean, occasionally I see swimmers floating, completely relaxed, carried along by the waves. Are we not swimming in an ocean of God and is not our only responsibility to release ourselves to It? In meditation we should have the same sense of complete relaxation that we feel when we are stretched out on the surface of the water, enjoying it and being supported by it. The Spirit is underneath and in us, and around us are Its everlasting arms, enfolding, protecting, and leading us forward as we rest effortlessly in the Spirit, giving ourselves over to Its sustaining waters and feeling ourselves carried forward on an ocean of love.

To remind ourselves in meditation that we are upheld by the waters of Spirit and floating on them will relieve us of all mental effort. Too much meditation is pure mentalism, an attempt by will power to storm the gates of heaven. While there is no denying that meditation requires effort, the effort is that of releasing ourselves to the Spirit in which we already live and move and have our being. If we do that many times a day—twenty, thirty, forty times if possible—we will have established ourselves in the Presence and will be caught up in the rhythm of God, just as we are caught up in the rhythm of the water when we are floating on it.

Alarm Clocks

Every opportunity to rest in the Spirit should be seized upon. It might be for a minute, perhaps for two. There is no specified

I, italicized, means God.

length of time, because time is a human measurement. It is important, however, that meditation not be a struggle, a burden, or some kind of a chore we perform out of a sense of duty. Instead it should be a living experience that continues throughout the day.

In order to make it that, a group of students followed a program of practicing the Presence which extended over several months. During the first week of the program, every morning upon awakening, the student was to begin the day contemplating the nature and activity of God, realizing that this is God's day and that it is not he who is to be glorified but that God is glorifying Itself as him.

The second week the student was to hesitate at every threshold he was about to cross and remember: "The presence of God goes before me to make the way straight and to be the love that greets me." Later, as a part of the program, after crossing each threshold he was to add: "The presence of God remains behind me as a blessing." That was all. Not every student was able to remember never to leave a room without that conscious recognition, and some of them had to go back and go through the doorway a second time.

One student who had driven halfway to work remembered that he had forgotten to remember. He had the courage to turn around, go home, and risk being late that one time. Another man went into his office, sat down at his desk, got up from his chair, turned around, left the office, and then came back quickly because he had forgotten to remember the Presence as he walked through the doorway. For several days he kept repeating what to his secretary looked like a senseless routine. Before long, however, it became an established habit to remember that he was not going through life on his own power but that the Presence was with him every step of the way.

Anyone can follow this simple program, and three weeks of this practice should result in a measure of proficiency. Some students may be tempted to think this is too simple for them and, therefore, a waste of time. But those who are willing to follow the procedure will feel as if they are almost falling into the Presence, living, moving, and having their being in God.

The fourth week, when the student went to his particular job —whether it was to sit at a desk and answer mail, work on an assembly line, or push a vacuum cleaner—he was to remind himself: "God brought me the work of this day, and He performs it." This should bring the awareness that the work being done is not the work of a person: it is God's work. So if the work is vacuuming the house, there must be the consciousness that He within appointed that person to do the vacuuming and, therefore, it should be done with joy and thoroughness. If the work is dictating mail or keeping books, He within brought the mail and He answers it, or He brought the figures with which to work and He adds and subtracts them. In this way the student learns to watch God doing the work through him, and he thereby becomes an *observer*, a *witness*, a *beholder* of God in action, key words in our spiritual ongoing.

In subsequent weeks the student was asked to see through the human appearance to the son of God at the core of each and every person. He was to express gratitude silently before taking a bite of food, recognizing that God is the spiritual substance of the food and that the table is filled with the bounty of God's grace expressing and appearing; and he was to remember every time he entered an automobile, an airplane, or any public conveyance that God, the divine Intelligence, is the only driver or the only pilot, and that the automobile or the plane is in the student's consciousness, maintained by his awareness of truth. Thus for more than seven weeks the activities every person carries on throughout a normal day served as alarm clocks to keep these students aware and remind them to practice the Presence.

Shortly after I began to meditate I became aware of the value of these brief moments of renewal. At that time I was a schoolteacher, and whenever there was the slightest sign of any unrest or disturbance in my classroom, instead of calling the class to order or saying anything at all, I closed my eyes for probably less than a second. It was so brief a period that it was more nearly a blink of the eye, but that infinitesimal pause was my way of recognizing that the infinite divine Intelligence, Something greater than my little self, was on the field. The interval was so short that there was no time for any words, yet it carried with it a world of meaning for me.

At the end of the year, the teenagers in my class were informally evaluating their teachers with one of my colleagues. According to one of my fellow teachers, when my name came up the comment was, "She is so patient, but—her impatience is growing!"

"What do you mean?"

"Well, whenever she gets impatient, she just closes her eyes, and she's been closing them a lot lately."

Be that as it may, it was magic. Just a second is all that is necessary to bring to conscious awareness the power and presence of God—just one second. A practice of this kind can be useful not only in the classroom but wherever we are dealing with other people.

Human beings are in the deep slumber of humanhood, and whatever leads a person consciously to remember the presence of God serves as an alarm clock to awaken him and keep him awake. Usually we think of an alarm clock as awakening a person at the beginning of the day, but the mesmerism of the world is such that alarm clocks are needed throughout the day. If we are tempted to forget the spiritual nature of our being, these alarm clocks, if kept well wound, will help keep us awake.

After we have tried seriously and for a protracted length of time to be aware of our oneness with the Source, we will be living in the conscious awareness of God. Then when we sit down three or four times a day for a deeper period of meditation, it will be for the purpose of communing with and enjoying our relationship with God. That is really what meditation is all about. Throughout the day by means of the alarm clocks of daily activity we will never stray far from the Presence, but in our periods of deeper meditation there is an opportunity for real communion.

It is important never to force meditation. Some students unfortunately work at it so hard that it becomes a mental activity, a kind of hocus-pocus, instead of a resting in the Spirit. Our responsibility in meditation is to provide the time, setting aside minutes during the day in which to open the door to let the Spirit reveal Its omnipresence. We are waiting and listening for an impartation from within, but as long as our attention is on people or things outside, spiritual impartation is buried in the noise of the world.

Even in the midst of a full program of teaching, I found it necessary to have those few minutes of meditation. Fortunately I had some unscheduled periods during the school day in which I was free to do whatever I chose. One side of my room consisted of a glass door and glass windows looking out into the hallway. What was going on inside could easily be observed by the constant stream of passers-by outside, who might think it strange to see me sitting at my desk with my eyes closed.

To the right of the glass door and windows, however, was a cupboard, and when its doors were open, I could sit in front of it without any concern about being observed. It was not long before that cupboard with its open doors became my holy temple where I could meditate in peace and quiet. Then whenever anyone opened the door of my room, I immediately became very busy straightening the boxes on the shelves. Never did a cupboard have so much straightening and yet look like such a total mess!

Anyone can find a spot in which to meditate, even if it has to be a cupboard. The important thing is to have a sanctuary, some place where occasionally during the day you can forget the whole world, turn within, and listen for the Presence which is always waiting to impart Itself.

Contemplative Meditation

Patience is required, for there is no predicting when there may be an inner response or when the awareness will come. But it will come. It may come the very first time we meditate. Then again it may not come for months. Every time we sit down for the purpose of being in the presence of God, we have fulfilled our responsibility. That certainly does not mean that we carry our burdens or our problems into meditation and use that period as an opportunity to let the mind go around and around, meditating on our problem and hoping for a solution. The very thought of gaining something of a material nature from meditation is a denial of God.

The purpose of meditation is to touch the Spirit within, that *I* which is always knocking at the door of our consciousness for recognition, but which all too often we fail to hear because we are so busy centering our attention on getting the meat that perishes and the bread that quickly becomes stale and moldy. When we live out from the Center within the manna falls fresh every day, the waters do not dry up, and we live on the invisible meat of spiritual consciousness.

When we look at something intently, trying to see and understand its essence, we are really engaged in contemplative meditation in which the mind, using thoughts and words, attempts to penetrate to the core of what we are contemplating. Thinking all the thoughts we can about a given subject, eventually we arrive at a point where there is nothing more to think. The principle is to still the mind, not by force or by will, but by coming to an end of thinking. It is similar to doing such strenuous physical labor that, when nighttime comes, the laborer falls into bed and scarcely moves again until awakening the next morning. So, too, we wear down the mind, not by consciously trying to do that, but by working with a specific subject as thoroughly as possible, so that afterwards the mind can settle into a quiet, peaceful state. In that moment of stillness, the Presence takes over.

In contemplative meditation it is helpful to take some principle, some question, or even a single word and examine it from all aspects. At first that may bring the same sense of helplessness it brought to a student who wrote: "When I received your first letter saying that I should just work with the question, 'What is God?', I was certainly nonplussed to say the least. I felt as if I had been taken by helicopter, per your orders, dropped on a desert island, given the principle of the backstroke, and told to think about it and swim home."

When we tackle a question like that we may come up against a blank wall, but if we persist, more and more of the nature of God will come to us, and it will not be merely words from a book. For example, the principle "God is law" might be words found in a book. But as we contemplate it, the meaning becomes clearer. We gain a glimpse of the truth that we do not have to bring that law into activity: it is forever in operation, maintaining and governing our affairs according to divine order and justice. Something begins to percolate in our consciousness.

In my first two years with The Infinite Way I meditated every morning, every noon, and every night on one subject: "I and my Father are one." Two years may seem a long time to continue meditating on the same subject, but my teacher had instructed me to use that scriptural passage for my meditation, and since he never gave me any further instruction in that regard, I continued and persisted. At the beginning it was a very halting sort of thing, like a baby taking his first steps, falling down and then picking himself up. Every morning I opened my meditation with "I and my Father are one," and waited. When in some meditation periods nothing came, I thoughtfully repeated those words several times. I did not repeat them in an attempt to make them come true but simply as a reminder that my oneness with the Father was already established.

At first nothing came, and I had to hold my attention to "I and my Father are one." Extraneous thoughts, totally unrelated to the subject, came barging into my meditation. But I would bring myself back to "I and my Father are one." Then my meditation might be interrupted by some noise outside. Again I came back with "I and my Father are one."

After going over that statement several times, my attention was finally arrested by the word *one*. What does it mean to be one? What does *oneness* really mean? I thought of the oneness of the flame with the fire. And I remembered the example of the wave and the ocean given in *The Infinite Way*.* I contemplated how the waves merged with the water: there was no place where the waves began and the ocean stopped, for they were one, inseparable and indivisible. All the qualities of the wave, its chemical constituents, were the same as those of the ocean. The color of the wave was the color of the ocean, and there was no way of separating them.

The same inseparability and indivisibility that is true of the wave and the ocean is true of my relationship with the Father. All that the Father is, I am; and all the qualities of the Father are my qualities because of my oneness with the Father.

And what is the Father? Do I really know? I have read about Jesus speaking of God as the Father, but what really is the Father? Do I know this Father?

Then it came to me one day that *Father* must mean the creative Principle of life. It was as if a flood had been released in consciousness:

I and the creative Principle of life are one, one and inseparable. There is no place where that creative Principle leaves off and I begin. I embody within myself all the creativity of the Principle of life because of my oneness with the Father.

*Joel S. Goldsmith, 10th ed. rev. (San Gabriel, Calif.: Willing Publishing Co., 1961), pp. 97–101.

Later it came that the Father is divine consciousness, the totality of awareness.

The Father is the divine consciousness, and I am one with that Consciousness. I am one with total awareness, instantaneous awareness of all that is. I do not have to attain it, because I already am one with all the wisdom, all the activity, all the knowledge, all the intelligence of that Consciousness which is total awareness.

I am one with the Life-force which permeates all life and all being. In that oneness, I, too, am the beginninglessness and endlessness of that eternal Being.

So as the weeks and months passed, more and more unfolded. I left the first word of the quotation to the very end. It was a long time before I began to ask: What am I? When I turned to what I am, I began to see that the *I* that is one with the Father cannot be a physical body. It cannot even be a mind. It must be of the nature of the Father, and therefore it must be the same Consciousness. It must be as incorporeal and spiritual as the Consciousness with which it is one.

I, my individual consciousness, and I, *the divine Consciousness, are one and inseparable. I am one with incorporeal Being, and my being is just as incorporeal as the divine Being with which I am one.*

I am one with that Presence which is here and there and everywhere, and I, too, am omnipresent being. If I am omnipresent, there is no place where I am not. Omnipresence fills all space.

Each time I began the meditation it was always with "I and my Father are one," followed by a period of waiting. If nothing came, it was repeated, not as an affirmation, not to make it come true, but simply as a reminder of something that already is true. At times something new would come, maybe just one little gem, one little facet of awareness. There might be long periods when nothing really new opened up. Nevertheless I persisted. For me,

"I and my Father are one" was the bread of life, and I turned to it to reveal whatever was necessary for me to know.

Experience has taught me that it is important to take one idea and stay with it for quite a long period of time even though there may seem to be no breakthrough on it. If we fall down in meditation because we seem to get nowhere, not even to a state of unknowingness, we have to pick ourselves up over and over again.

The Fruits of Meditation

Contemplative meditation takes us beyond words and thoughts, not by resisting them, not by fighting them, but by using them. Then, when a point of inner stillness is reached, we are at peace. The mind is quiet, and we are open and ready for whatever is to be given us. Probably most of the time there will be nothing, nothing we can know with our mind, nothing we can hear or see, but because we have opened ourselves to Its operation It is working in us and through us. At the most unexpected time, in the midst of the most so-called unspiritual activity, an idea may pop into our mind which is the perfect answer to a problem or direct guidance to making a decision—whatever we may need at that particular moment. Since this did not happen while we were meditating, probably because we were looking for an effect, we sometimes do not recognize it for what it is: the fruitage of the meditation. We have fulfilled our part, however, when we take time to open ourselves to the Presence, trusting Omnipresence to reveal Itself in whatever way is necessary.

The meditation is complete when the mind stops racing around and there is a stillness, which may not last for more than a moment. God knows nothing about minutes or hours. It is that moment of conscious contact that is important. True, the contact is always there because never is it possible to be separated from God, but it is in meditation that *conscious* contact is made and the little self communes with the one and only Self.

At times there may be a sense of hearing a voice, of being immersed in light; even a vision may come. But let us never be deceived by any of these effects and, above all, never seek for any kind of an effect. Many persons who have visions and hear voices have never experienced God. The visions and voices that they see and hear are mental projections, all on the level of mind, the level of good and evil.

In the beginning stages of my practice of meditation, I was very much impressed and somewhat amazed at the stories some people told me of their "experiences." Two women who came to see me said that whatever they wanted instantaneously materialized before their very eyes. Because I was puzzled by this I wrote to my teacher, recounting the incident and telling him that I really had no right to be helping students with meditation when I did not have such "experiences." His answer was very much to the point, "Look at the fruitage!" And I looked. There was no fruitage, none whatsoever except increasing confusion and depletion, which made me realize what a vast difference there is between a mental activity and a spiritual activity.

We can always know how successful our deep meditations are by the fruitage. What kind of fruitage? The automobile we want? The new house we would like to have? No, indeed. We will know it by the peace we feel within, the love that is flowing out from us and through us, the joy, the renewed sense of life. These are all fruits of the Spirit. Amazingly enough, they translate themselves into what is sufficient for our daily needs. But that comes only when our motive is pure and we are not going to God to get our will accomplished. We are going to our Source for the joy of being in communion with that Source. That is the reason, and there is no other reason.

It is not difficult to determine on what level a person is functioning. If a student experiences some particular phenomenon in meditation and there is no fruitage of a constructive nature, but rather disturbance and inner turbulence, he can be assured that it is not of the Spirit. The fruitage of the Spirit is peace, love, and joy, which are then translated into the outer experience.

We never seek any effect in meditation. Even if we should have an experience of seeing light or hearing a voice, and it is a true spiritual experience, that still is not God. That is the effect of God. We should never be content with an effect, but should rejoice in every beautiful spiritual experience and then let it go, never trying to hold on to it. God can reveal Itself today in one way, tomorrow in another, and to the end of our days in ever new experiences. If we are intent on recapturing some experience we will surely lose our way, an evidence of a lack of understanding of the infinite nature of God and God's infinite ways of expressing Itself. We should not seek to grasp and hold on to any *form* of experience. What is necessary to seek is the silence within.

At first that total vacuum of absolute silence does not come very quickly, and often it is of short duration, but that vacuum, immeasurable in time, can work wonders. It is that nothingness, a resting on no thing, on nothing that can be defined in any way. It is then that we have opened the door for the Spirit to impart Itself to us. Impartations and even revelations may come through in those moments. When these take the form of words and thoughts, it will be the Spirit within doing the thinking and the meditating. That is pure meditation. In such moments we rise above words and thoughts and go beyond what we already know. We may not be able to put into words what It is imparting at the time, but from the fruitage we will know that we have received the Word.

There are times when we turn within and immediately feel the warmth of the Presence, the awareness of Something greater than ourselves. We are speaking with the Father, and the Father is speaking to us, and that is communion.

Conscious union, however, is a deeper experience in which there is no longer an awareness of ourselves *and* the Presence. In conscious union there is no personal sense of Self: there is only One. With some that conscious union continues for an extended period of time. Most persons who do attain it, however, are unable to maintain it because they come under the hypnotism of good and evil and are thrust back into the world. Through contemplative meditation they must find their way back again to conscious union.

At one time in the depths of the despair that comes from a sense of barrenness, I found myself crying out, "Oh, God, just speak to me."

Like a flash the answer came, "Would you speak to yourself? *I* am the only Self there is, and *I* am right here."

The ultimate in meditation comes when we no longer have any awareness of a separate identity or of our meditating as a person. There is just the Spirit revealing Itself as all. This is union. God is being "you" and God is being "me," and we are swallowed up in infinite Beingness. Then we move about just living and being, not even conscious of meditating, and yet we are meditating all the time, for we are in that Consciousness, and It is expressing as us. It carries us forward through the world. Each step of the way It takes us, and we never have to think about what we would like to do or what we would like to have. This within us that is our very own being knows all, and if anything is needed for Its fulfillment, it appears so instantaneously that many times it is there before we can think about it.

The silence of meditation is not the silence of a graveyard; it is the silence of a garden growing. There is no deadness in a garden, but in that all-pervading silence an intense activity is going on in the ground which will later take form as buds, blossoms, and fruit.

So, too, in meditation there is not a blankness, but a rhythmic activity of Spirit. The silence of meditation cannot be attained by will power, so never try to blank out the mind. As the mind exhausts itself the Spirit comes through, and we are in the kingdom of heaven. True, we are still on earth, our feet are solidly on the ground, but the ground is not the mire and dirt of human experience; it is the holy ground of spiritual awareness.

When we discover the kingdom of God within, we behold the miracle: this earth is heaven. Our whole point of view changes: we see the world with new vision because we see beyond what the eye sees, beyond the visible to the invisible substance. The mind has become a limpid pool of water that mirrors a perfect universe.

3

Be Ye Transformed

And be not conformed to this world: but be ye
transformed by the renewing of your mind, that
ye may prove what is that good, and acceptable,
and perfect, will of God.

Romans 12:2

Probably as long as we walk this earth there will be times when
we look at some form or effect and are momentarily gripped by
fear. It is possible, however, to come through most of the difficult
experiences we are likely to encounter unharmed if we maintain,
with steadfastness, the awareness that there is That within us
which walks with us through every circumstance and every experience. Then, whatever the problem, it will be faced without fear.

With every problem comes the opportunity to change what is
at first only an intellectual awareness of a spiritual principle to a
real conviction. Frequently the same type of problem presents
itself over and over again, providing an opportunity to attain
enlightenment in that particular area.

The parenthesis in which we live might be likened to a school,
which means that, as in every school, there are lessons to be
learned. There are certain persons, situations, or conditions to
which we react and to which we give power to cause us discomfort
or unhappiness. But just as a child must experience putting two
and two together many times before arriving at the understanding
that two and two are four, so sometimes we have to work through
a particular type of problem over and over again until we reach
the consciousness of its nonpower. Then we are free.

Some persons seem to have difficult recurring physical problems, recovering from one ailment only to have another appear,

then another, and another one. Uppermost in their minds is their most recent illness or hospital experience. Then there are people whose body gives them little or no trouble but who go from job to job, always finding someone with whom they "simply cannot work." Others experience lack, and even though the supply comes it does not last. Still others move from one unhappy experience to another.

If each person could look at himself objectively and recognize the particular area of human consciousness that is constantly reasserting itself as a problem and learn to see through it, he would no longer react to it with fear, concern, or anxiety. These problems would fade out of his experience. We all have work to do on ourselves, and that work is to see through the suggestions that present themselves as conditions or persons.

Big problems are not always as difficult to surmount as little ones. Do we stub our toes on a mountain or on the little rocks along the path leading to the summit? Is it not the little day-to-day irritations that cause us to lose our way? Are we not usually able to rise to meet the big problems that face us? When we work with the principles of spiritual living and spiritual healing, especially the principle of oneness, in the more or less unimportant situations, a consciousness develops which makes it possible to avoid many of the big problems. Gradually a quiet assurance, an unimpeachable authority, and an inner beauty become ours because of our steadfast abiding in oneness, despite the problems we face.

When the knees of a cypress tree are injured by some wild animal pushing against them, perhaps a boar with its tusks or a deer with its antlers, it is those bruised knees that become the most beautiful of all. If there were no rocks in the little brook it would just flow along and much of its beauty would be lost. The rocks make it sing. Just so, those persons who have used spiritual principles as guidelines to work through their problems show forth a special richness in their experience. The song they sing is purer, deeper, and more melodious. So each problem offers us another opportunity to develop that depth of consciousness that can sing above the noise and inner turmoil that the problem engenders.

From the Caterpillar State of Consciousness to the Butterfly State

When we are on the human level of consciousness, sometimes the simplest happening looms as a very real and difficult problem. Is that not somewhat like the experience of the caterpillar as it slowly creeps and inches its way along the ground? When it comes to a huge log, a formidable obstacle and barrier to the caterpillar, it climbs over it laboriously. To the caterpillar state of consciousness, the trunk of the felled tree is a problem to be surmounted. But when the caterpillar feeds for a certain length of time on milkweed leaves and goes into a period of relative inactivity or silence, it enters the cocoon stage. In the darkness and peace of the cocoon the caterpillar form is finally left behind. What emerges is the form of a butterfly—a beautiful insect whose gauzy wings bring it freedom to fly as it will. It is the same life, but having now realized its freedom it is able to fly right over the log, which is not the same barrier to the fetterless butterfly that it was to the earthbound caterpillar.

So it is with us. All the components that made for a situation of inharmony may still be present, but when we emerge from the caterpillar state of consciousness into the butterfly state, that is, when we rise in consciousness, we are able to fly above the problem and be untouched by it. It evokes no reaction in us. Problems that before were difficult barriers are no longer problems. A higher dimension of consciousness has been attained, and we live above the problem.

In the butterfly state of consciousness a lightness, untouched by the problems of the world, is achieved. We have risen high enough to recognize a problem for what it is. As long as it remains a hard solid condition, situation, or person, we are stuck with it. But when the lightness or clearer perception of the butterfly consciousness is attained, the problem no longer touches us. When spiritual healing is experienced, what really takes place is that we are transformed from caterpillars to butterflies. Through the realization of Omnipotence, Omnipresence, and Omniscience, we rise in consciousness to the place where the things of this world no longer act as power in our experience, and there is nothing to be overcome.

If there is only one Presence and if we see discord or inharmony, what are we looking at but an image in thought, a false concept of that one Presence? To rise above that we enter the cocoon stage, going into the silence in which an activity of consciousness makes us consciously aware of the one Power ever present. Just as the butterfly emerges free, no longer bound by the caterpillar state of consciousness, so are the scales removed from our eyes, and instead of a sick body, a lacking pocketbook, a disordered mind, or an unhappy relationship, divine perfection is revealed.

Attaining a Conviction of One Power

In order to reach that stage, we engage in the study and contemplation of specific principles, working consistently with one principle until a conviction of its truth is attained. Whatever the principle with which we are working, it cannot be merely up in the head: it has to be lived. It is not enough to hear about a principle, to read about it, or even to meditate upon it, although that is important. But what is the point if, for example, in meditation we blissfully realize the nature of one Power and then immediately become frightened about something that claims to be a power in our experience? Fear of the things of this world arises out of the belief that they are power and that they can do something to us. Would we fear appearances if we knew in our hearts that they are not power? Is it not because we think they are power that we curl up with fear?

At one time a man asked me to state in a few simple sentences what I considered to be the most important spiritual principles so that he would have something to work with. I set forth briefly the basic principles necessary to develop the mystical conscious- ness: God as *I*, pure Spirit, all-embracing Love and Wisdom, infinite Being precluding the possibility of any other being; God appearing as individual being; and the nature of "this world" as appearance. At the same time I gave him the statement "God is the only power" as a specific principle to be used for his medita- tion, study, and practice.

Several years later when he came for an appointment, out of his wallet he took a little worn piece of paper on which was written, "God is the only power." He went on to explain that it had taken seven years for that principle to take root in his con- sciousness, but at last he was beginning to catch its significance and understand it. Seven years! And some persons think if they work with a principle for five minutes they are ready to flit on to the next one.

It really does not matter much with which principle we begin. If we take the principle of one Power, we might ask ourselves in meditation what one Power means. To each person different aspects of its meaning may be uppermost at the beginning. The first thing that might come is that God, the Infinite Invisible, is the only power, a statement which everyone would probably ac- cept. But then, seeing all the persons and conditions in the world that claim power, must come the questions: What about the power of disease, accident, lack, and death? Is there power in external things, persons, and events? Where is power? With suffi- cient contemplation will come the realization that all power is in the invisible, divine Consciousness which is also our individual consciousness; therefore, whatever claims to be a power out in the world cannot in reality be a power in our experience.

On my second trip to Hawaii a little six-year-old child came to visit me. While swimming, she had been bitten by some sea creature that made her itch continuously. As she scratched and scratched she was trying to realize that what she was experiencing was a false concept—a misinterpretation of what was really there—and that it had no power. She kept reminding herself: "If you can see it, hear it, feel it, taste it, or touch it—it isn't!"

What really is, is that invisibility which can never be known through the senses. If we are tempted to believe that there is some power in form or effect, it is up to us to recognize that the only power there is, is within us: unlimited, pure, perfect, and undefiled Consciousness. In the realization that power is in the invisible Consciousness, we are no longer victims of material laws or beliefs. No power external to us can operate upon us if we have sufficient awareness of this truth. But how often do we claim that there is no power but God, the divine Consciousness individualized, and then in the next breath give power to food, disease, or some person, almost immediately forgetting that all power is in the invisible Consciousness which we are?

If we can learn to look at everything we see, no matter how beautiful, how ugly or terrifying, and steadfastly recognize that there is no power in it for good or for evil because Consciousness—God—is the only power, realization will come. Can we see God with our human eyes? Can we hear God with our physical ears? Can we touch God with our hands? Can we know God in any way through the physical senses? No; God, Spirit, is invisible, and invisible Spirit is the only power. Power, then, is not in what is visible; power is not in what we see: power is invisible.

Accepting this premise, we can withdraw power from whatever we are aware of through the physical senses. If we realize that the things of this world have no power to do anything to us, that they cannot limit our life, curtail it, interfere with it, or end it, why be concerned? To know those words will not make the so-called powers of the world nonpower, but when a conviction comes from the depths of consciousness, never again will there be as great a temptation to fight anything as a power.

Knowing that evil, whether it appears as disease, lack, discord, dishonesty, or sin, is not power in the realized presence of God eliminates the inclination to fight it, enabling us to stand still in the light of spiritual power which reveals what *is*. In the darkness we walk around blindly groping our way through a chaotic world. When we learn to be still and let the Power within flow through us, that stillness is the light which dissolves the darkness. Shadows or distortions of the spiritual universe and the spiritual body disappear, just as when the sun is at its zenith, straight above, there are no shadows.

It is said that when the darkness that dwelt in a cave heard about the light, it became so curious that it journeyed out to discover for itself what light is. But the light so dazzled it that it hastened back into the cave.

Then the light asked the darkness, "Show me your darkness." The darkness invited the light into the cave. When the light entered the cave, it said again, "Show me the darkness." But there was no darkness!

There never is any darkness where the light of truth is shining, just as in the presence of spiritual power realized there are no other powers: no powers to overcome, no powers to resist, no powers to fight. When the darkness is gone and the shadows have been dissipated, the spiritual universe is revealed in its perfection and wholeness.

In the silence, this truth is realized. It is not usually possible to attain that stillness, however, until we have worked for a period of time with some one principle, such as the principle of one Power, until we arrive at a consciousness of it so that we know that there is nothing with which to struggle.

If the problem that is disturbing us persists in going around and around in our mind during our contemplative healing meditation, that is when the principle of oneness—one Power, one Life, one Law, or one Substance—is needed to lift us into that higher consciousness where silence reigns, a silence so great that the earth melts. It may last for only a fraction of a second, but all that is necessary is one or even less than one second of total and absolute silence, for spiritual power to rush into the vacuum and for the light, which that power is, to reveal that there is no darkness and there are no distortions or shadows.

A Better Concept of Body

How many times are we presented with the suggestion that some part of the body has deteriorated? That is the time to lift consciousness by adhering to the principle that there is only one Substance, the invisible spiritual Substance which never deteriorates or disintegrates but is always perfect, whole, and complete. That is the substance of the body, formed by Consciousness out of Itself.

Through generations of human belief the concept that the physical sense of body is our body, that it is born, matures, ages, and finally dies, has been accepted. But that is only the belief, the counterfeit, the shadow. The spiritual body is the real body. It is the only body we have, and it is here and now. We do not have a spiritual body *and* a physical body: there is *one* body, the one spiritual, indestructible body which is the pure instrument of Consciousness.

What we see is a concept of the one spiritual body, an image in mind—not *our* concept, but a universal concept which explains why everyone sees much the same picture. The concept or picture is what we try to heal until we awaken to realize the truth that there is nothing to heal, nor is there any condition to change. If we attempt to change a condition, we are trying to change that which has no real existence. Even if it were made better, it still would not be the spiritual body.

One of the toughest problems we encounter is that of the body, which at times seems to be our real master. When we have an ache or pain, fear immediately takes possession of us. Sometimes it may be a very subdued and almost hidden fear, but back of the ache and the pain is the fear.

We must stop identifying with the physical sense of body if we want to develop the mystical consciousness of oneness. We must stop believing, when the body aches, is in pain, or presents some appearance of malfunctioning or disintegration, that that condition can destroy life. Life formed this body and Life maintains it. If we work with the principle of one Life for a sufficient length of time in enough different situations, the day will come when there will be a conviction that there is only one spiritual and indestructible Life. With that conviction as a part of our consciousness we would never fear for our life. The absolute conviction of such a principle constitutes a measure of illumination.

To experience the dominion promised us in the beginning, it is necessary to understand who we are and the real nature of our being as consciousness. Intellectually we know that there is more to us than the body we see and use. Probably most of us have a sense of ongoingness even when we see a body stretched out before us, inert, and to all appearances a corpse, because there is within us the feeling that life is continuous.

Life, Beginningless, Ageless, and Endless

Although we admit that God is life, we completely negate that principle when we become afraid for our life. If we really believed that God is life, could we fear for that Life? Would we fear for the life of God? Surely God knows how to maintain Its life appearing as us. Can anything ever destroy the indestructible life of Spirit?

If we decide to work with the principle of one Life, then in a contemplative meditation we might ask: What is life? What is the nature of the Life that is God? What is spiritual life? That, however, is not enough to make the principle of one Life come alive in our experience. We have to live it. How? By applying that principle in every situation. For example, is not birth as much of a challenge to the everlastingness of life as is death? So when the appearance of birth is presented to us, then is the time to realize the birthless and beginningless nature of life.

When confronted with the appearance of death, we must "be instant in season" and remember that there is no life to die; there is no life to lose because the only Life is God. To think it, to read it, or to say it is meaningless unless we apply the principle in every situation by never accepting the suggestion of a life beginning, a life ending, a diseased life, a helpless life, or an aging life.

How easy it is to get trapped into thinking that the years are slipping away and that we are less vital and not as strong as we once were! So subtle is that suggestion that unconsciously we accept the belief that we do not walk or hear or see as well as we did when we were younger. Infinite Way students must come out and be separate and not be fooled by these appearances. As we persistently refuse to accept every untoward suggestion or appearance as the truth, we begin to experience the fullness of life regardless of how old we are according to the calendar.

Life does not need to be renewed. It is forever expressing its fullness, and that does not imply a decrepit, aging, lessening, weakening life, but the life Jesus referred to as "the abundant life."

Life, being God, is invisible, so we can never see Life although we do see the effects of It. You and I are invisible consciousness. True, we have a physical sense of body, but we are not that body: we are that invisibility which nothing can touch. The flames do not burn that Life; the sword does not pierce It, because that Life is God. God has given Its life as our life, and It is indestructible and invisible.

To gain the consciousness of the principle of one indestructible, invisible, spiritual life, we must consciously and constantly disassociate ourselves from the body and understand that the body is ours in the same sense that the house in which we live is our home. Still we are not the house. So, too, we have a body which serves as our instrument, but we are not the body. The body is ours, and in reality the body, too, is indestructible because the body is formed by Consciousness and is of the substance of Spirit.

Is it not clear how much is involved in the one simple principle that God is life? What wonders that would do for us if we lived and practiced it! We would need nothing more, because every time the temptation came to think that some disease was appearing in our or someone else's body, immediately would come the realization that we are invisible spiritual being and that none of "the fiery darts of the wicked" can touch the Life that we are. We come under material laws or beliefs merely because we have accepted the universal belief of a physical sense of body. None of these laws or beliefs we think of as affecting Life ever really touches Life. That Life, being God, could not possibly need healing. What needs healing is the physical *sense* of life we think of as ours, and that healing is brought forth by awakening out of all physical sense.

Instead of accepting such suggestions as: "Oh, that poor old soul!" or "That poor sick thing! Isn't that too bad!"—suggestions which are a complete reversal of the one Life which is God—we should meet them with the principle of the invisible and eternal nature of Life. We cannot develop the consciousness of the one Life in a minute. It is the faithful practice over weeks and months and years that brings about that transformation of consciousness.

If we are reacting to some situation and the mind is in turmoil, we quiet it by contemplating one Power, one Presence, or the principle of one Law. With practically every problem some material sense of law is involved, whether a law of disease, an economic law, or legal law. We remain anchored in the truth that just as the one Law maintains the perfect balance in this universe so does It maintain a perfect balance in the spiritual body. Spiritual law does not operate upon us, is not outside us, nor do we bring it to us. We embody the Law that maintains the balance, harmony, and perfection of our being. That Law is an infinite intelligence which knows how to govern according to divine wisdom and is always operative as the experience of those who are consciously established in It.

Problems Can Be Stepping Stones

A problem should be looked upon as an opportunity to gain a greater awareness of whatever principle we may be working with, so that we can testify: "To this end was I born, that I might bear witness to the truth of the infinite, indestructible nature of Life and Its perfection. That is why I am here: to be a witness to the divine perfection." We need never be ashamed of the problems that come, because they are opportunities. But that does not mean that we should accept problems as necessary or desirable, that we should remain in them or become bogged down by them. Instead we should use the principles as alarm bells to awaken us out of the problem.

I am not this body that was born in a certain year and will eventually rest under a tombstone: I am the eternal, birthless, deathless, and invisible life. Nothing material can touch the invisibility that I am.

I walk through this world, in it but not of it, unafraid because I know that whatever would interfere with the life I am knows nothing of that invisible life and can never reach it.

As consciousness of the principles develops through our contemplation of them and our bearing witness to them, we react less and less to problems. Realizing that God is our very own being, never again will we try to reach out for a power, because we can rest in the awareness that God, omnipotent, omnipresent Consciousness, is individual consciousness. In reality, the divine Consciousness individualized is the substance of all that is and governs every aspect and area of our life. Into that pure, perfect, undefiled Consciousness no element of discord, disease, disaster, or decay can enter. Until we understand God in that light, however, we will always be struggling and trying in some way to become what we already are.

Consciousness does not have its seat in some part of the body. It is not in the body. Rather, the body is cradled and nestled in Consciousness. Consciousness is eternally maintaining Its instrument, and no destructive activity or force of any kind can penetrate it. We take possession of the body when we release it to the Consciousness that formed it, which knows precisely what is necessary for the perfect functioning of Its instrument.

My body has no power to act of itself. The muscles cannot move or contract or expand of themselves. The lungs cannot function of themselves, nor can the heart beat of itself. The Consciousness that I am moves the muscles. The Consciousness that I am maintains every organ and every cell in their right relationship one to another so that there is no such thing as malfunctioning or misplacement. The divine Consciousness which I am knows how to maintain Its own creation, rebuilding, revitalizing, strengthening, and activating even that which appears to have been destroyed.

A Contemplative Meditation Reveals Isness

A contemplative healing meditation is much like seeing a beautiful landscape. We look at the landscape and take in a bird's-eye view of it. But as we continue observing it, we see new things that at first escaped us: a boat perhaps, a different kind of tree, some flowers, the ever changing sky. As we gaze at the landscape, we are not struggling to create a tree or to change the sky. We are simply looking at it, enjoying it, and becoming increasingly aware of various aspects of it. So a healing meditation is contemplating and enjoying the wonder and miracle of God, not trying to create anything, not trying to change one small part of that landscape. Instead we are absorbing it, taking it all in. With such contemplation comes a beautiful sense of peace as we feel the effortless activity of the universe permeating the scene. We are beholders of it, but we did nothing to create it.

This is a very significant point. When we look at the landscape, we make no effort to change it, only to see it as it really is. That is exactly what we do in a healing meditation. We contemplate God, Its perfection and completeness. We do not contemplate the person needing help because there is no person in whom there is anything to change. Whatever is, is that infinite Consciousness, that immutable law and ceaseless activity of God. Our responsibility is to become aware of It and to bear witness to It.

It is important to approach a healing contemplative meditation in a relaxed way rather than to think: "Now here is a situation I must do something about." If we try to change a person or condition, we are likely to go at the problem with hammer and tongs, struggle with it, mentalize, and probably end up with a headache and a stiff neck. What we are called upon to do in our healing meditation is to contemplate God, just as we contemplated the beauty of the landscape. As we center our attention on that beautiful landscape called God, all the truth that has been revealed to us in the days, weeks, months, and years of meditation comes into focus.

God, the activity of each and every moment since the beginning! From everlasting, God has been the only activity going on. God is the only activity going on now; and God will be the only activity going on forever. There is no time when and no place where anything can begin that does not proceed out of the activity of that divine harmony. For that reason there is no moment when any evil or any error can begin. There is only the unlabored activity of Spirit expressing Itself as the activity of the body. There is an eternal rhythm to Its peaceful, ever present activity, a rhythm of rest and movement, but never a struggle or conflict.

Spirit is the substance of which this universe is formed, a Substance into which nothing of a harmful nature can enter to disturb, to irritate, or to infect. There is never too much Substance and never too little. That Substance is divine intelligence, forever as perfect as the Spirit which It is.

How great is the peace of beholding the landscape of God: God as activity, God as substance, God as peace, God as the law which maintains Its own, each in its own orbit! As I become aware of God's activity unfolding and revealing Itself as order, perfection, and love, I am at peace.

When faced with a problem, we drop the problem and immediately turn our attention to the one permanent reality: God, the Presence within. If nothing comes, we sit quietly reminding ourselves of the word God and what we know about God:

God, the only Presence, the All-presence. Right here where I am in the midst of this temptation is the presence of God, the presence of life and peace.

God, the divine Consciousness which I am, is the only power. In the presence of Its omnipotence, every claim to power fades and dissolves before Its light, in which there is no darkness. This light is the very substance of the body, nothing less than perfection itself.

Every activity of the body is governed by that same spiritual law which maintains the balance and the equilibrium of the universe, holding the planets in their proper sphere of activity, tirelessly and effortlessly. The same yesterday, today, and tomorrow is this changeless and eternal law. It is wisdom itself, a wisdom which knows and maintains the right relationship among all things in the spiritual universe.

The body is held and embraced in my consciousness, and my consciousness of the truth of one Power and one Presence maintains it in its wholeness and completeness.

This meditation remains entirely on the level of spiritual reality, never dealing with any person or any problem and never coming down to the mental picture, the concept. We contemplate the principle of one Presence, one Power, one Consciousness, and one Law, and we stay with the word *one* until we reach a state of peace. No matter how many words come through, the real healing takes place when there are no more words, only silence and a sense of release in which we can rest.

Soon after I embarked on the spiritual path, I realized that it is not enough to read about the principles of spiritual living. They have to be practiced. That presented a dilemma. My few personal problems offered me little opportunity for extensive practice, so I began to observe the persons around me: friends, relatives, and neighbors. Then, as I studied the faces of the people I met on the street, I was reminded of Thoreau's observation, "The mass of men lead lives of quiet desperation." Truly, those who live in this world without a star to steer by often walk a weary way. Everywhere I looked I saw abundant opportunity to apply the spiritual principles I was studying.

Although my ignorance was colossal, there was one principle which really registered with me: God appears *as* individual being; God constitutes individual being. This became my yardstick, my measuring rod. Established in that truth, I began to recognize the spiritual identity of the persons around me. I did not meditate for them in the sense of trying to change some condition or trait of character, but the problems which appeared to be overwhelming them pushed me into a realization of the spiritual identity of each one as the beloved son of God and all that implies. With that principle I worked day after day despite the fact that no one asked me for any help with his problems. In fact nobody was at all impressed by anything I knew, and I might add that nobody received much help. But these problems were a challenge to me, and I kept practicing and practicing and practicing.

Was all that effort wasted? Not at all! The principle of God as individual being began to take root in my consciousness, so that after a year and a half of practice when a stranger called on me for spiritual help, I was ready. How did I know I was ready? Not only from the fruitage, but because there was no reaction in me to the problem. I was not concerned; I was not afraid; I was not thinking, "Oh, what shall I do now?"

It is not necessary to know a great many truths. One truth realized will plant our feet—at least one foot—right in heaven, but it has to be a realized truth. Realization does not come without dedicated and consistent work, which translated means without a dedicated and persistent activity of consciousness.

Attaining the Mystical Consciousness

Often the very simplicity of truth misleads those who are unable to understand that the deepest and greatest mystical truths are the simplest. The mystical consciousness rests on the solid foundation of the simple but clear-cut principle of oneness. It is not a nebulous consciousness which, like a cloud, is tossed about by every wind that blows. To attain the mystical consciousness, the principle of oneness must be so lived that it becomes the very fabric of our being.

It is inconsistent to have a beautiful meditation in the morning on a principle such as one Power—realizing that there is no power outside to act upon us but that all power flows out from us—and then go out into the world and accept as power the barrage of suggestions that are thrown at us. If we do that, we are a divided household, believing that there is a spiritual life and a human and material life. And there isn't! There is only the spiritual life and the spiritual universe here and now.

Many persons who have an ache, a pain, a serious disease, a dire lack, or gnawing unhappiness turn to a spiritual teaching for healing, not realizing that the purpose of a spiritual teaching is not to change bad into good, to make a sick body well or a poor person rich. That is all on the level of the pairs of opposites. The purpose of a real spiritual teaching is to lead the seeker into the kingdom of God within, into spiritual consciousness where there is neither sickness nor health, neither lack nor abundance, but pure spiritual being which to the human being is indefinable.

In the human state of consciousness, problems are undoubtedly very real and powerful. It would be utterly ridiculous to say that there is no power in a deadly disease or a tragic accident, when on the human level of consciousness these things obviously do have power. In everyone, however, there is the divine urge toward perfection which is the reality of being but which has not yet been fully realized. That urge appears as a desire for healing, but it really is an urge pushing us forward to greater awareness which eventually will result in a transformation of consciousness.

It has been said that consciousness must be transformed, but in reality it is not consciousness that has to be transformed: it is awareness that must be expanded to realize the infinite nature of that consciousness. We are pure infinite Consciousness, but at the present moment, not having fully realized that truth, we live as limited states and stages of awareness of the one Consciousness. None of us has as yet fully realized his own infinity or his own divine nature. Instead of struggling to change the outer picture, we should be willing to labor for days, weeks, months, even years to bring about what loosely can be described as a transformation of consciousness, although it is in fact a removal of the veils that hide the perfection that already is.

The transformation of consciousness comes with discipline and a dedication to spiritual principles. The ultimate approach to spiritual healing and living is to reach the point where the problem elicits no response regardless of what it may seem to be. There is no attempt to change the concept. Instead there is a resting in the mystical consciousness of oneness which has been attained through working with spiritual principles in many different situations.

Probably many will say, "I don't know what to do when I am faced with a problem. I feel so inadequate." I hope you will always feel inadequate. There is no better time than this moment to underscore this truth: *no human being will ever know how to heal.* Considerably different from a state of inadequacy, however, is complete confusion and fear. A sense of inadequacy rightly understood is a willingness to relax and rest and wait. Wait for what? For an impartation from within, for the Word to be given us, the Word that becomes flesh.

The first temptation when faced with a problem is to dwell on the problem and think, "How I hurt!" or "How I ache!" This is the time to use the spiritual principle of oneness to lift us out of that mesmeric sense. The principles, the words and the thoughts we are thinking, and the contemplative meditation in which we review the truth, never heal anyone. But the contemplative meditation is important because through the truth we contemplate we reach that state of consciousness which can be still.

"Be still, and know that I am God." To repeat that statement does not bring about a stillness, but a deep contemplative meditation can lift us to a point of such stillness that it can move mountains. It is not our words; it is not any truth we know. Rather, it is the truth that flows forth from within us, God speaking and imparting Itself when we are listening. But how can we listen when we are burdened with some pressing problem? So our real problem is to get to the point where we do not contemplate the problem.

Through our working with the principles, a wave of stillness and quietness overtakes us, and that is it. It is necessary, however, to return to that flow of truth again and again, ten, twenty, thirty times a day and for ten, twenty, thirty, forty weeks. I hope not for forty years, but what are even forty years in eternity?

Each time the meditation will be different, but it must always be on the level of God. Sometimes nothing at all comes, and so again we say to ourselves, "God! God!" The words do not matter. What matters is whether or not we are getting closer and closer to the sense of oneness, for that is the mystical consciousness which knows there is nothing to be changed, nothing to be healed, and nothing to be risen above.

Healing is an important aspect of the discipline of the spiritual path because, through healing, the mystical consciousness of oneness is developed. Coping with the problems of the world through the application of spiritual principles in day-to-day situations is the catalyst which transforms knowledge into awareness.

Healing is becoming aware that the divine activity which is

now in operation is governing every moment of our life and the life of the whole world. That is the truth, but there must be a conscious awareness of it. When the realization comes, we are living in the same world, yet it is different. We do not see it the same way, and people are different, too. We have emerged from the caterpillar state of consciousness and, like the butterfly, soar above the temptations of this world which appear as problems. The unfettered and free nature of pure Being is coming into sharper focus.

4

The Dragon Shalt Thou
Trample Under Feet

Thou shalt tread upon the lion and adder: the
young lion and the dragon shalt thou trample
under feet.

Psalm 91:13

To most people healing means bringing God down from the
heavens to make a sick body, a sick pocketbook, or a sick relationship whole. But healing according to the principles of The Infinite
Way has nothing whatsoever to do with changing conditions or
changing human evil into human good.

Many persons misunderstand this aspect of spiritual principles.
They assume, because we say we are not interested in changing
human conditions, that they are supposed to go on being miserable, suffering, or dying. That is not what we mean at all. In the
human sense of world, disease, death, lack, unhappiness, and
limitation are real problems, and many of us suffer from them.
But when we are able to rise to a higher dimension of consciousness, to the butterfly state, the problems of this world are no
longer power and bring forth no reaction in us.

Contemplating God, the nature of God, the nature of the
spiritual universe, and the nature of the spiritual body help to free
us from the temptation to accept something as a power which is
not power *in the realized presence of God.* The contemplation
itself is not power either, but it serves to lift us to a place of
silence. In that silence where there are no thoughts and no words,
the Presence reveals what eternally is.

The statement that healing can be brought about with a smile
is true. It is also true that when a person reaches the stage of

working problems in calculus, he needs none of the earlier steps in mathematics which took him up to that point. So it is with this idea of healing with a smile. Unfortunately, too many students lose their way because they are unwilling to take the necessary preliminary footsteps.

Perhaps one of the greatest bugaboos in the spiritual ministry is that everybody wants to be so advanced. Many times we have to begin at the very beginning and remind ourselves of the nature of God, the nature of individual being, and the nature of error. We need never apologize for being beginners or having to sit down many times during the day and night, and sometimes take the "forty days and forty nights" apart from the world to meditate in order to gain the spiritual discernment that sees through the bubble of world belief and breaks it. Far more serious is the attempt to live out from a state of consciousness which has not yet been attained.

The first step in dealing with a problem, whether our own or someone else's, is to drop the problem and the person as quickly as we would drop a hot skillet to keep from being burned. Whatever form the meditation takes, it must never be a contemplation of a problem or a person.

If we are not supposed to think about the person or the problem, how does he receive help? What are we to do? What we are to do is to reach a state of peace by realizing all the truth we can remember, not the truth about the problem, for there is no truth about the problem. Even though we drop the individual and the problem, a contact has been established with the person who has asked for help. In coming to our attention, and more especially if he has asked for help, he has made himself a part of our consciousness, which is a consciousness that knows there is only one Self, one *I.* That *I,* appearing infinitely, is the *I* of the person who needs help and is already perfect, complete, and whole. Our awareness of the infinite perfection in which there is no person other than that *I,* God appearing as individual being, and in which no discord of any kind can operate is the light which reveals that there is no problem.

While there are many different kinds of healing meditations and many different ways of approaching a problem, one way is to contemplate the various facets of oneness as pointed out in the preceding chapter. If the person or the problem begins to push in upon our consciousness, we come right back to God: God, the one Life; God, individual, infinite, eternal, everlasting Life. The more we work with a particular principle, the more unfolds and is revealed about it. Through persistence in meditation, truths that we have never read or heard about will be revealed.

A student on the spiritual path knows that his function is to lift a person above the human experience, not only above bad humanhood but also above good humanhood. In fact, good humanhood probably poses the greatest struggle of all. Is it not true that when we enjoy good humanhood we are usually content to rest in it? The Spirit within has a way of prodding us, however, until it pushes us to the point where we are not content to rest in humanhood but are forced to move forward until we find ourselves home in God. To be home in God is not merely to be a better human being. To be home in God is to "die" to the human sense of good and the human sense of evil.

On my first Infinite Way lecture trip to Germany a young woman came to me, unjustly berating and condemning herself for certain omissions in her past relationships. After she had finished talking, we meditated, and I waited for the right words to come. Suddenly out they popped: "Whenever you begin to think about this particular problem, just say to yourself, 'Drop dead, Margaretta, drop dead!' " meaning, not that she should cease living, but that she should "die" to her human sense of self.

A month after this experience, Margaretta made a surprise trip to Zurich for my class there. She came up to me beaming and all smiles, and in much better English said, "Drop dead, Margaretta!" pointing to herself and adding that whenever the sense of guilt came upon her, she met it with those three words. She had begun to "die" to the human self, which is the only self that knows any struggle. The struggle that most of us experience comes because the little personal sense of self is determined to be in the ascendency. It wants to be catered to and pampered. If we were willing to slough it off and let go of it, our problems would be greatly lessened.

Understanding the Nature of the Problem As Appearance, Suggestion, or Temptation

Even with dedicated, consecrated practice, we still may not have achieved oneness with our Source. Something is missing. What is missing is that we still have God *and* a problem. Deep down, unconsciously, we are looking to see if God has done anything about the problem. Although most of us believe we are too advanced to fall into such a trap, nevertheless most of us look for an improvement in the condition which is troubling us.

This brings us to one of the most important healing principles of all. Because of the infinity of God and Its goodness, the nature of the problem must be an appearance, a misinterpretation of the eternal goodness of God. There can be all kinds of appearances. For example, does it not appear that you and I are sitting fairly still without much movement? But actually we are hurtling through space at a terrific speed as the earth turns on its axis. If we were able to grasp the speed with which we are moving, we probably would become dizzy thinking how fast we are going around and around. An appearance is not what *is*. In spiritual healing it must be understood that the problem is an appearance or suggestion, and a suggestion does not make a thing real.

While no one word will be adequate to every situation, anything that makes us realize that the problem has no real existence is worthwhile. For example, the word *temptation* can be used to describe the universal belief that we can be separate from God, have a life of our own, and that there can be a substance that can cause pain or suffering; whereas in reality there is only one Substance, one Life, and one Being. The temptation that comes to all of us is to believe that there is something other than God at the center of our being, God as the very *I* that we are.

Jesus responded to the suggestions that came to him with: " 'Get thee behind me, Satan.' Get thee behind me, temptation. I cannot be made to believe that there is any power or any life other than the One." If we could respond to every temptation in the same way and really have a conviction of its truth, in all likelihood the problem would be less acute. But that would not be what had really happened. What had really happened was that more and more of the divine perfection was revealed.

There is another word for the problem that may ring a bell. If we can understand that whatever the problem appears to be is caused by a sort of hypnotism,* we have it licked, because hypnotism never creates anything real. We can be hypnotized, if we consent, to believe almost anything, but that does not make it true.

For example, suppose I am hypnotized while having tea with friends. I am made to believe that the door opens and a tiger, its fangs bared, walks stealthily in and looks right at me, knowing that at last he has found his next delicious morsel. What would I do? I would probably get out of the chair just as fast as I could and run, not caring if I knocked over my friends, the tea table, or precious bric-a-brac. My friends, who are not hypnotized, would look at me in amazement, thinking, "What ails her?" They would not see any tiger. The fact that I am hypnotized into seeing a tiger does not make a tiger. Do you not see that hypnotism creates only an impression, a suggestion that something is that is not?

As human beings we are all hypnotized in a measure by the belief in good and evil, laboring under some measure of the hypnotism of world appearances. But the substance of what we

*For a further discussion of this subject see "What Did Hinder You?" in Joel S. Goldsmith's *The Art of Spiritual Healing* (New York: Harper & Row, 1959), pp. 56–69.

see is hypnotism, a mental image, a mental concept, which has only the substance of mind.

Stripping Aside the Debris of Universal Belief

The mind that accepts two powers can be called the universal human or carnal mind. A seven-year-old friend of mine to whom the word "carnal" had no meaning whatsoever called the carnal mind the "caramel" mind. Instead of getting stuck with the "caramel" mind, which is nothing but the belief in two powers, get unstuck and let the mind take its rightful place as a pure instrument for the Spirit.

The carnal mind is the mind that is filled with judgments arising out of the belief in two powers. A mind filled with truth, however, is a clear transparency for the spiritual universe, revealing the spiritual body in all its perfection and the world in its spiritual essence.

This is a spiritual universe, but we see it "through a glass, darkly," that is, we see it through a mind that over generations has been trained to believe that some things are good and some things are bad. The carnal mind constantly judges and evaluates, not in terms of reality but in terms of pictures and mental images. It sees only a concept of the spiritual, perfect universe and the spiritual, perfect body, which needs no healing and no improving.

When Michelangelo was asked how he could have made anything so unbelievably beautiful as his statue of David, he is said to have responded that the statue was already there in the stone. All he had to do was to chip away the extra stone, and when he had chipped away enough there was the statue.

We are already that perfect being which needs no healing. All we need to do is chip away the debris that hides it. That is healing. Healing will not take place, however, as long as we believe we have to change something. Instead we must realize that an appearance does not have to be changed but only seen through.

Our problem is to clear out the generations of beliefs that have clouded the mind and made it a poor and inaccurate transparency. How is this accomplished? By feeding the mind with truth, with spiritual wisdom and spiritual literature, rather than with trash from sensational newspapers and those paperbacks, movies, and TV broadcasts which portray all the drivel of human beliefs. When we begin to feed the mind with truth, concepts are cast off one by one, enabling the mind to become sufficiently still so that an impartation from within, the Word, can emerge and become the flesh of our experience.

The Word heard in the stillness melts the fleshly concepts. "He uttered his voice, the earth melted." What earth? The conceptual one. The earth that we see as the solid physical earth is the earth of concepts, but when we hear the Word within, which may never be heard as a voice but which may come as an awareness, then the earth melts: the fleshly concept is burned up. Does it change anything out here? No; rather the concepts the human or carnal mind has been entertaining are dissolved, and instead of seeing a *concept* of the spiritual body or the spiritual universe, in a moment of silence the real body and real universe are seen.

At first this awareness appears outwardly as improved concepts. The body may seem younger, healthier, stronger. This is still only an improved concept, but in a moment of illumination the spiritual body, which is not a concept at all, is revealed. It is the body that we have had from the beginning and will have a million billion years from now, for we will always have a spiritual form which is indestructible, painless, and weightless. This awareness does not come in a moment, but when we catch clearer and clearer glimpses of what really is, the concept improves as the mind becomes more and more a transparency.

The body we see is mind-formed. It is not solid flesh and blood but mind forming itself in terms of its concepts. Right where the physical sense of body appears is the one spiritual body. The physical sense of body is a picture in the mind. That is why we never deal with physical conditions. What appears as a physical condition is mind forming itself as a picture which must be erased through the transformation of the mind.

As long as we believe that we are faced with some deadly disease, it will be difficult to reach a state of peace in meditation. But when we recognize that what we face is a mind image, because matter is mind formed, then we can settle down to realize the nature of the spiritual universe and the nature of the spiritual body right here and now. Through this we are able to cease struggling and to reach a state of peace. The only purpose of knowing the truth is that we may become so convinced of the reality that our mind becomes a mirror showing forth the perfection of the divine Consciousness which is individual consciousness and which forms itself as the body.

It is possible to develop a state of consciousness in which whatever is presented to us—all the horrors this world would throw at our mind—brings forth no response in us. The only way that can be done, however, is to see the problems for what they are. And what are they? The carnal mind, mental images passing before us.

There is only one carnal mind, and that is why we all see the same picture. Oneness is a principle that must never be forgotten. There is only one Consciousness, and in reality there is only one mind, which is the instrument of that Consciousness, a facet of It. In belief, however, there are two powers, and that belief in good and evil constitutes the carnal mind. We all come under it, in a measure, until we awaken. Sadly enough, most of us awaken in one moment but then go to sleep again, until pain or some other problem nags at us and forces us to dig deep down within to awaken.

Mental Pictures or Concepts Never Change
the Eternal Reality

It is important to remember that we are never faced with anything but mental pictures. Mind forms itself as pictures that look like hard, solid matter, but the pictures we see never change the reality that is there. When I was in Lausanne, my hotel room overlooked Lake Leman. Across the lake were breathtakingly beautiful mountains which I looked forward to seeing every day. But when I awakened one morning, the mountains had disappeared, and in their place were heavy dark clouds. Did the clouds do anything to the mountains? Did they remove the mountains or change them? Never!

So, too, the fact that our mind is racing around, creating all kinds of pictures, never changes the eternal reality. It never changes our body; it never makes it sick. It never changes the infinite abundance which is ours. No! Clouds, mirages, hypnotism, or the carnal mind with its beliefs of good and evil never change one tiny portion of reality even though to us the mirage, clouds, or hypnotism may seem very real—and they are real as long as we are on the level of mind and matter.

Only when we rise in consciousness to that place where the mind becomes a still pool of water, a perfect mirror, do we see reality, the reality which does not need to be healed. What we see in our unillumined state is the misperception of the divine reality, whether it is called the carnal mind, appearance, suggestion, temptation, or hypnotism.

There is a vast difference between *believing* that a thing is true and its actually being true. Hypnotism never creates anything or any condition, so when we are faced with a problem, it is important to recognize quickly that the only substance the problem has is appearance or hypnotism. Because of universal hypnotism we accept the belief of disease. But let us never be fooled into believing that hypnotism has made the disease. It has not. Again, hypnotism never creates anything: it only creates the belief in things. Hypnotism never changes the spiritual universe and spiritual creation. It never changes oneness. It never creates duality or twoness.

Eventually we reach the stage where we would never think of dealing with a condition of the body or with a person. At first we might be tempted to do so, but the time comes when we instantly recognize that what we are faced with is the carnal mind, appearance, or hypnotism. When the hypnotism is broken, the whole world of material sense—this *sense* of a material world and a physical body—is also broken.

Sometime ago a student sent me a delightful little poem:

> The whole world moves in a mishmash mess.
> It moves not out of its own not-ness.
> But let this strike the Isness stone,
> I ask where has the not-ness gone?

Yes, this whole world is a mishmash mess, a grand mess, mesmerism which is a form of hypnotism. And where has the not-ness gone when *Isness* is touched? It never was. Healing work will be more effective when we begin to work with the principle that whatever we see, good or bad, is hypnotism and without power.

Many times there may be the temptation to delve into the human picture to discover what the claim is and what caused it. That is not the way. In order to meet the problem there must be the immediate recognition of the condition, not as a cancer, not as lack, not as pneumonia, but as hypnotism. We are not dealing with a condition: we are dealing with hypnotism. Hypnotism is the substance of the problem. Knowing that, we can rest in the realization that hypnotism never creates anything.

The Problem, a Universal Hypnotism

A student once called me to say that her child had a severe case of pneumonia. It had reached such a critical stage that the child's lungs were filling up and it appeared that she might go on.

Now how should I deal with that? I don't know anything about pneumonia and I don't know about lungs and I don't know how to heal anything. Should I begin to realize that there are no lungs to fill up or there is only one kind of fluid? No, the first thing that came to me was that this is a threat to the life of God appearing as individual being. Anything that is a threat to the life of God would have to be hypnotism, because there is nothing that can touch the life of God. This is a picture being presented, not to the mother of the child, but to me, a picture of pure and simple hypnotism. Hypnotism is the only substance of the appearance, and there is nothing to do about hypnotism except to see through it and to recognize it as hypnotism. All I knew was that this was a temptation for me to accept hypnotism.

I asked the mother to call back in a short time. In about two or three hours she called and told me that immediately after she had spoken to me, the child grew worse. Then she went on, "My child coughed and coughed and coughed until she was practically torn to pieces. I thought each cough would be her last. Finally she coughed up a metal staple, and almost at once she was all right." It was not pneumonia at all, not even from a human standpoint.

Suppose I had been meditating to heal pneumonia? Would that not have been fruitless and stupid? What good would it have done? Since this was not pneumonia, all the prayers and all the meditation in the world to heal pneumonia would have been of no avail. When the situation was recognized as hypnotism, the hypnotism was broken and the whole problem dissolved.

This experience proved to me once and for all that we should never deal with a condition. If we do, we are caught up in the hypnotism. It is not a condition we face. What we are faced with is a universal hypnotism. Our work is to realize that since God— infinite Being—is appearing as individual being, there is no person to be hypnotized, including me. Thus I cannot be hypnotized, either. I am the only one with whom I am dealing, because I am the one being presented with this picture. I have to realize that there is no mind that can be hypnotized, no mind that can believe in two powers: the only mind that exists is the pure instrument of God.

One reason many persons have so little success in healing work is that they are trying to change a condition as if it were real, instead of recognizing that it is a false mental concept of what is really there. Hypnotism is the substance of all the ills from which the world suffers. It is vitally important never to forget that hypnotism does not create anything except the temptation to believe that there is a condition or a power other than God.

The world of God's creating is here and now. The person of God's creating is here and now. What we see with our senses is the conceptual world, the world of hypnotism. It is not God's creation at all. Seeing through a muddy glass produces a distorted picture of what really is, but when the glass is a clear transparency, the divine harmony that already is and always has been shines through. To attain the consciousness of this principle, it is necessary to practice seeing through every appearance, always remembering that there is no *person* to be changed, nor is there any *condition* to be changed. We must be the ones who are not hypnotized. One unhypnotized person, standing fast on the principle that God is all and that there is nothing else, can dehypnotize a whole group of persons.

To celebrate Halloween, a doting mother placed a fearsome witch mask on her little daughter, who pranced around the room practically swooning with delight as her brothers fell back in simulated terror. Then she went running down the hall to find her father so she could frighten him, too. She burst into the bedroom and stopped dead in her tracks in front of a full-length mirror, numb with fright at the image confronting her. When her father quickly pulled off her mask, with a great sigh of relief she cried out, "Oh, it's only Debbie." We, too, are frightened when we see tuberculosis, cancer, pneumonia, unemployment, unhappiness, and lack. But they are the masks universal belief has fastened on us.

How can there ever be union, conscious oneness with God, when the masks of universal belief stand between us and God? When we recognize this world of appearances as hypnotism, however, we can see through the mask right into the heart of the spiritual universe. Then there is nothing to desire or to seek, and we are at peace, abiding in that inner kingdom.

Our God is so great, so infinite, and so omnipresent that there is no room even for a you or a me. There really is no "you" or "me": there is only God. We are one with the Father, and in our oneness with the Father we recognize only the one Self, the one Life. Because we have seen through the hypnotism, we behold God's universe and the glory of that universe.

Anything that can be known with the physical senses is a form of hypnotism. The real, the eternal, the everlasting divine creation, which is God expressing Itself as all that is, can be known only through spiritual discernment. As our eyes are opened to the divine reality, we realize that there are no persons or conditions that need to be healed or changed.

Every evil condition is a temptation to accept some power apart from the power of God. Every problem is a call upon us to remember that right where we are is the spiritual universe perfect, complete, and whole. If we are seeing less than that, we are the ones who are hypnotized, and it is incumbent upon us to wake up until we are living constantly and continually in that atmosphere of peace, love, and wholeness which is the kingdom within. We stand fast in the liberty with which the Christ has made us free. And in what way has the Christ made us free? By revealing Itself as our spiritual identity, as the son of God.

To work with every problem as hypnotism, a nothingness, a nonpower, or a nonsubstance takes us into that mystical consciousness of oneness where there is not God *and,* but only God: God appearing as individual being and God appearing as the spiritual universe. The spiritual universe is not up in the sky some place, not even up on a mountaintop. The spiritual universe, made of the substance of Spirit, formed by Consciousness and maintained by spiritual law, is right here. In this spiritual universe there is no disease, no lack, no limitation, no unhappiness, no discord, no human being: no one to be healed and no one to be changed. There is only the reign of divine harmony and a peace that is all-pervading, which nothing can disturb. Whether we can accept it or not, we are in that spiritual universe now. We do not have to go any place to find it. It is right where we are. Therefore, let our prayer be:

Open Thou mine eyes that I may see and behold this spiritual universe. Reveal Thy glory here and now. Do not let me try to change the universe: let me behold it.

Nobody can really explain how healing is brought about. But those of us who understand these principles and have worked with them until we could become sufficiently still have witnessed miracles of healing, regeneration, and reformation. Except for those few who come into this world with a healing consciousness as a gift of Grace, it takes practice to attain it; it takes work. It does not come by wishing, nor does it come by merely reading or repeating words. The words we use are for one purpose alone: to lift us to that place where we know that there is nothing besides "My kingdom." In that kingdom there is no consciousness of disease, lack, and unhappiness, and we do not look around to see what has happened to them. They have ceased to have any reality or existence for us after we have attained the consciousness of oneness.

The mystical path is not a way of meditating on one Power and one Presence for ten or twenty minutes and then going out into the world and forgetting about that oneness. It is the way of constantly recognizing the presence of God wherever we are. It requires alertness every second.

Through constant practice, these principles eventually become so much a part of our consciousness that we can never be convinced of any power other than the one Power. This is similar to becoming proficient in any art. For example, if a pianist practices the scales, one day he will make music, and no longer have to think about scales and notes. He will not be consciously aware of them, yet music will be flowing forth. We can all be music makers when we are convinced that there is one Presence, one Power, one

Life, one Law, and that anything contrary to that oneness is hypnotism or material sense.

What if it takes twenty years to attain this consciousness? Will they not be twenty years well spent? Every bit of spiritual consciousness that we attain is ours forever, and since truth is infinite, that awareness will be unfolding and revealing itself forever in new ways. So far we have caught but a glimpse of these principles. As we work with them and witness the fruitage time after time, the awareness will grow, the conviction will come, and we will be satisfied.

5

In His Own Image

God created man in his own image, in the image
of God created he him; male and female created
he them.

Genesis 1:27

Many fairy tales contain deep spiritual lessons. An example is the
story of Hansel and Gretel, which Humperdinck used as the
theme of his tuneful and colorful opera. Hansel and Gretel had
been sent out into the woods to gather strawberries, but instead
of obeying the instructions given them by their angry mother,
they romped about having a delightful time, completely forgetting the work they were supposed to do. Suddenly the darkness
was upon them, and when they were unable to find their way back
home, they became terrified because they remembered that this
was the forest in which the wicked witch lived.

In one performance of the opera, sinister-looking trees had
been placed on the stage in the distance as the background to set
the tone of the play. As the trees moved menacingly toward the
children, coming closer and closer, their fear became more and
more overpowering. It was as if the trees were imprisoning them,
leaving no way of escape. At that moment a fairy appeared and
put them to sleep, an even deeper sleep than that of humanhood.

When morning came, there, set in the midst of the trees that
had appeared so terrifying the night before, stood a little house
made of the kind of material that would captivate children: gingerbread. Decorating the house and serving as ornaments were
small gingerbread men, the epitome of human good in the eyes
of children. Out of this charming cottage strode the wicked witch,

greeting the children and gloating over these new victims she could bake in her furnace. Although Hansel and Gretel were already under the witch's spell, they were still alert enough to discover that the witch, despite her magical powers, was nearsighted and hard of hearing. So, as she opened the door of the oven to throw them in, they crept up on her and pushed her into the oven where, in a burst of flames, she was burned up.

And then what happened? All the victims she had hypnotized, fashioned as gingerbread men, and baked in the furnace to entice other victims came alive again. Once again they were children dancing around, proving that their real identity had never been altered. Under the witch's mesmeric spell, however, they had forgotten who they were and thought they were gingerbread men. Powerful as the wicked witch seemed to be, she never was able to change or touch the real self of her victims. The two children, with the little awareness they had, could turn on the witch and cast her into her oven. Then what was she? Nothing, just nothing but a mesmeric belief in a power apart from God.

Sometimes, as I sit answering my mail or the telephone and read or hear about all the pictures of discord, lack, and disease knocking at my door, I can't help but think, "Gingerbread men! just gingerbread men!"

Fear acts like a vise, making us feel as if we are held tightly, almost immovable. Is there any vise to hold us? Or is the fear but another gingerbread man? Even though it looked as if the children had been changed into gingerbread men, their essence or reality was never touched. We are able to understand this as we begin to awaken and see that what appears as power out in the world of effect is really without power and without substance to a realized spiritual consciousness. Whatever the problem under which we are laboring, the life, love, and peace which are an integral part of our being are never touched by the personification of the illusory sense of twoness, appearing as the false sense of Self. The *I* that we are remains pure undefiled Consciousness.

God has given us His divine consciousness as our individual

consciousness. Since the nature of that divine Consciousness is infinite, can there be another? That Consciousness in Its fullness is ours; it is the Consciousness of our friend and the Consciousness of our enemy, a Consciousness that can neither be hypnotized nor destroyed. What we see as friends or enemies are mesmerized gingerbread men, but they are as unaware of their hypnotized state as are we.

With the realization that there is only one Power, the appearance dissolves and is gone. Where? Gone back to where it began, back to what it was in the beginning—nothingness: no power, no substance, no law, no cause, and no effect, always a universal mesmerism. It is not your mesmerism or my mesmerism. It is a *universal* mesmerism. The *I* that we are cannot be mesmerized, so never do we say, "How I am hypnotized! How I am mesmerized!" Can the divine Consciousness appearing as individual being be hypnotized? Is it not malpractice when we say, "I am hypnotized"? The truth is that *I* cannot be hypnotized. Why? Because the *I* that we are is the beloved son of God, and the son of God can never be hypnotized. The "I" that can be hypnotized is only a false sense of *I.* If it is a false sense, it cannot be a real person.

So let us be through once and for all with the belief that the *I,* which we are, can be hypnotized. If such a suggestion should come to us, we should wake up and recognize: This is too ridiculous! We do not fight hypnotism; we do not struggle with it. If we all had a sufficiently good sense of humor, particularly about ourselves, we would be able to go further on the path much more quickly. Too many of us take ourselves and our problems too seriously. Why not laugh at ourselves, especially at the suggestion that God as individual being can be hypnotized or have any personal sense, that is, have the *sense* of a person separate and apart from God Itself—even though that is the appearance.

Our work is to reveal the spiritual identity of every person. That revelation appears outwardly as healing, but in reality it is becoming free of the concepts that hide what *is.* Every problem is the carnal mind. But whose carnal mind? The only mind there is, is the mind that is the instrument for the divine Consciousness, a pure transparency for God. So there cannot in reality be a carnal mind.

Impersonalize the Problem

No matter what the problem is, we must first lift it out of the person in the sense of separating the belief from him and putting it where it belongs in the carnal mind, which is just a bag of wind, a nothingness. And what is nothingness? One child's response to that question was, "It's a balloon with the skin peeled off." With the skin peeled off the balloon, what is left? Nothing. That is the end of it.

The healing principle consists in knowing that only God is and that God is the only person there is. That person needs no healing. This that appears as an ailing or disagreeable person is the carnal mind, the balloon with its skin peeled off, absolutely nothing. It is never the person.

After a person has worked with this principle for a period of time and it begins to take hold in his consciousness, he is set free from trying to help or heal persons and from fearing some of them. As long as there is a person he is trying to help, he is fighting, resisting, and struggling. The fact that there is no *person* he is trying to help does not mean that no healing takes place. Instead better healing comes with the understanding of his own spiritual identity and the spiritual identity of every person.

The various problems that appear as persons are but the masks which universal belief has accepted as persons. But the mask is never the person. Recently a student wrote to me, "It strikes me as almost silly to think that I should express gratitude to some person, silly for it is so obvious that all gratitude belongs to God. However, if He chooses to disguise Himself so ingeniously and marvelously, I suppose there is no reason why I should not deliver

my gratitude to Him as He appears in one of His many disguises."
Then she went on to add, "Love to all the other disguises,"
meaning the other persons in the household.

Yes, we are all disguised, but it is not God that puts the disguise
on us. God is not disguising Himself. It is the sense of separation
which has led us away from our true identity that has placed a
disguise upon us. A person who is the instrument for spiritual
healing is the person who can see through the disguise, that is,
see beyond the appearance to what is really there and never hold
a person in judgment or condemnation, but always impersonalize
the good as well as the evil.

Putting the principle of impersonalization into practice calls
for a total surrender of judgment. We find this difficult because
we are so convinced that our judgment of a person is correct that
we are unwilling to see through the disguise to what is really there.
We cling with a tight grasp to these concepts of persons, nourish-
ing and nursing them and adding to the disguise by putting a few
more ugly marks on it so it becomes a little worse each time we
think about it, instead of stripping it aside and recognizing: This
is not a person. This has nothing to do with a person: this is an
impersonal suggestion or temptation coming to me. This is hypnotism.

As we are awakened out of the hypnotism, we see a person in
his God-identity. The remedy for all the ills of the world is to
awaken to the truth of spiritual identity. That is the only real need
there is. It is not necessary to remove lack or disease, because in
the infinity of God there is neither lack nor disease. It is not
necessary to find employment for a person, because God individualized is forever employed in being Itself. It is only necessary to
awaken to the truth, and we can better do that in proportion as
we impersonalize what is being presented to us.

Every problem always involves a person. The conflict that is set
up between persons has to be resolved within ourselves, not by
changing the person or looking on with a holier-than-thou attitude, murmuring to ourselves, "Look how hypnotized he is!" but

by impersonalizing the problem. It would be very comforting to be able to feel that someone other than ourselves is the hypnotized one. The principle, however, is that the problem is being presented to us as a person, and therefore we have to separate the problem from the person.

It will do us no good to meditate and then look up quickly to see how much the person has changed. Nearly always the temptation is to look for a change in someone else, never in ourselves. We think we do not have to change; we are already perfect. And we are! Yes, we are, but we are not expressing that perfection as long as we continue to see imperfection in others. It is up to us to see through every disguise, through the masks that we have accepted as our associates, friends, and enemies. It is up to us to recognize that God constitutes individual being, not only our individual being but the individual being of every person.

The Work Is Always on Ourselves

Nothing that appears in the form of a person need cause us concern. What we do need to be very much concerned about is what is taking place in us. If we react to a person with a feeling of love, hate, dislike, distrust, or fear, usually it is because we see in him the very qualities which, in our hypnotized state, we ourselves are expressing. If they were not within us, they would bring forth no reaction. Each of us can think of persons in our experience to whom we react and those to whom we do not react. If we react, it is almost certain that what we are reacting to is really some quality that our consciousness has mistaken for a person—as personal to us or to someone else. It has to be met within ourselves: we do not meet it in the other person, we meet it in ourselves.

If we see something that the world labels as evil and it draws forth no judgment or condemnation within us, no reaction of any kind, that usually indicates that we have already met that particular problem in this life or in some other life. We do not judge the evildoer or condone the evil deed. No matter what the situation is, we are never helpless. We can always get busy with ourselves.

A student who had felt a great surge of spiritual activity wrote to me that it had come to her: "Not only acquaint now thyself with Him and be at peace, but acquaint now thyself with Him and get busy." Yes, get busy; be active; do something, instead of sitting by passively. Acquaint now thyself with Him and get busy: get busy with meditation; get busy with the practice of the principles; get busy with your study. Do something, and the something we can do is to work on ourselves. It is possible to awaken if we are willing to recognize our own spiritual identity and that of the person who appears to need help, knowing that only the qualities and capacities of God can be expressed as any individual. Whatever discord appears as a person is an impersonal error which has no channel or avenue of operation. It is the nothingness of that balloon with the skin peeled off.

A very disturbed woman who was going to a counselor for help was asked after several visits if anything had happened to her or if she felt any better. Her response was, "No, I'm not a bit better. But everyone else is much nicer." Everyone is "much nicer" when we raise up his spiritual identity as the beloved son of God. But we are not bearing witness to the beloved son of God as long as we see and accept the faults of a person, his diseases or sins. Only when the mind becomes still and free of its concepts can the beloved son of God be seen.

What is it that we see as sin, disease, death, lack, or limitation? What but hypnosis, mind, false pictures? The whole substance of the picture is mind. And what kind of a mind? A mind in turmoil. When the mind becomes quiet, it becomes a clear pane of glass through which we behold the reality of all being.

The more we think about a problem, the more we perpetuate it. Since every problem is mind-formed, every thought we pour into it is like feeding the body the most delicious kind of chocolate cake. According to human belief, eating chocolate cake adds weight to the body. Dwelling on a problem adds weight to the mind, increasing the problem. It is like rolling a little snowball in the snow, making it bigger and bigger.

It is a mistake to think that the problem is due to our wrong thinking, and for that reason we are suffering. The problem is a concept in the universal carnal mind. Just as there is only one divine Consciousness which we are in our true identity, so there is only one carnal mind which functions in us as long as we are entertaining the belief in good and evil. When we are free from the belief in good and evil, the mind becomes still and is the transparency it was intended to be.*

Recognizing the Spiritual Identity of a Person

To understand that there is only one Consciousness makes the world new for us. Everything takes on a special glow, for we are looking out at the world with spiritual vision and beholding spiritual identity.

What a transformation that could make in our experience with people! What a surprise is in store for those with whom we come in contact when we no longer see them merely as human beings! While we are smiling and speaking the language of the world, we break the wall of separation by greeting those we meet with the love and joy we feel through our silent recognition of their Christ-hood. This should be made a specific daily practice.

The spiritual identity of a person, his Christ *I*-dentity, is the reality of his being. All the rest is a mirage, a myth, a state of self-deception, a disguise. As we recognize the *I*-dentity of others, our vision penetrates beyond the mist of personal sense, with its judgment, criticism, and condemnation, to what really is. Who can criticize, who can condemn, who would dare to sit in judg-

---

*For a further discussion of this subject, see "Transcending Mind" and "Unconditioned Mind" in Joel S. Goldsmith's *The Thunder of Silence* (New York: Harper & Row, 1961), pp. 63–78.

ment on the son of God which you are and which I am?

When we recognize the spiritual identity of a person, true oneness is revealed. This is love, the only love there is, the love that sees through the human mask of the name tag a person wears to the one great name *I*, recognizing this *I* as the only being there is.

I have no human parentage. My parentage is of the Father, and my inheritance is of that creative Principle which includes all. The traits of character I inherit are from the Father within.

It is the function of a father to provide the right environment for his offspring, so my Father, the creative Principle, has placed me in a spiritual environment which is never dependent on any thing or any person in the world. The I within me has created and formed Its own environment. The creative Principle of life is responsible for my education and receptivity and for leading me out of human beliefs into spiritual awareness.

I live under the divine authority and government of the Father, the government of truth, love, and justice.

All sin, disease, and death spring from the belief that we are human beings with a human heritage, possibly a good physical vehicle and possibly a poor one. But it is the Father within that formed and created us, that made the body of spiritual substance and brought us forth into being. That being has no human inheritance and is not subject to human beliefs.

When we accept no human origin but recognize the purely spiritual origin of our being, our Christ-self, we are free from the beliefs and suggestions of humanhood. This is rising into a higher dimension of consciousness in which there is neither birth nor death but only the eternality of that divine *I* which is forever revealing and expressing Itself.

PART TWO

BUILDING THE TEMPLE

6

Eye Hath Not Seen,
Nor Ear Heard

Eye hath not seen, nor ear heard, neither have
entered into the heart of man, the things which
God hath prepared for them that love him.
I Corinthians 2:9

At one time or another most of us have searched ourselves and
wondered: Why was I born? What is the reason for my living?
Why am I here? I didn't ask to come here, and here I am having
to struggle to make my way in a hostile world. Was all this just
a happenstance, and am I now out here on my own?

Those questions, which have plagued many of us, and their
answers have often brought forth only a greater sense of confusion
and frustration. Far too many of us lose what should be the joy
of life because there seems to be such a lack of fulfillment. A sense
of purposelessness pervades every activity. Yet, until we find our
purpose in life, there can never be that real joy of awakening in
the morning, knowing that there is a work for us to do.

All too few of us have found our unique function in life. We
came into this world for a reason, but we may have failed to
achieve our unique purpose because we have not been able to
extend our horizons beyond the limitations of our present experience. Several years ago when I was driving through the English
countryside with friends, my attention was arrested by a sign
which read: "He who cannot see the invisible will never do the
impossible." So, too, he who does not have the spiritual discernment to see beyond his limited sense of world can never recognize
the infinite potentialities of Consciousness to which all things are
possible.

Our tendency has been to think that it is our responsibility to decide what we should do, and therefore our energy goes into carrying out our human planning. This limits us to what we have learned in past experiences, so many of us never discover that we have a higher purpose in life. That purpose may involve something of which at the present moment we have no knowledge whatsoever.

As a child I learned a verse from the Bible which has remained with me and has carried me through deep valleys and up to mountaintops: "Eye hath not seen, nor ear heard, neither have entered into the heart of man, the things which God hath prepared for them that love him."

I could not have dreamed of the kind of life that has unfolded for me because I did not even know it existed. But the Self within me which is all wisdom knew how It could best be fulfilled as me, and when I became sufficiently quiet and was willing to surrender every desire, concept, and thought, this Self took over and led me by a way I knew not. It led me not out of this world but into a fuller and more complete activity. My mind could not possibly have conceived of the things that God, appearing as my individual consciousness, had prepared for me, because it knew nothing of the untouched riches of spiritual consciousness.

No one has any way of knowing what is stored up for him in the divine Consciousness until he turns within. I was reminded of this several years ago while riding hour after hour on a train from Chicago to Los Angeles, past barren hills and parched ground. As the train rolled through miles and miles of what looked like just so much wasteland, I speculated on the riches that might lie hidden in those hills and valleys, minerals and chemicals whose value man has no way of knowing at the present time because these riches and their use have not yet been discovered.

If we knew that somewhere in our backyard a diamond lay buried, we might spend hours, days, and weeks digging and sifting through every bit of ground to uncover it. How much more valuable a use of time would it be to spend weeks, months, or years sifting through the debris that covers up the treasure that lies within us!

Every person, whether at what is called the beginning of a lifework or in the latter years, can benefit by taking time to ask:

Father, what is Your will for me? I seek not my own, but Your will. Why was I brought into this particular experience? What is the divine plan for me? What is the spiritual purpose in my being here?

For weeks and months we may have to ask ourselves these questions in meditation, but the reward of doing it is considerable, because one day we will know that we were brought to this earth for a purpose and that our being here is no accident. Furthermore, a practice of this kind makes us receptive and responsive to the divine Intelligence which governs this universe and our experience, if we but open ourselves to It.

Is Failure Always Failure?

Our greatest problem is that we are seeking fulfillment for ourselves, a concept which must be given up. It was never meant that we were to be fulfilled, but that the divine Consciousness might be fulfilled as each and every one of us. In that realization, a great burden drops away. If we think of how we are to be fulfilled, that places a heavy responsibility on us because we may not know how it can be done. But if we release the responsibility to the divine Consciousness to be shown forth as us, it becomes Its responsibility to fulfill Itself, and our responsibility to be receptive to Its impulse.

Sometimes there has to be a tremendous emptying out before we understand the reason for our being here and are able to find our rightful place. This involves a surrender of our concepts of what we think we should be doing and a willingness to begin where we are.

Right where I am the presence of God is, and therefore right where I am is holy ground. I need look no further, but only realize that if this is not my place, I need have no concern because divine Intelligence is operating, and It will take me wherever I should be. I accept this place where I am now as holy ground, and I do whatever is given me to do this day with joy and gladness, realizing that there is Something within which has brought me to this point and that It is doing it.

Often there is an unwillingness to accept this truth until we are overwhelmed by a sense of failure. Sometimes what appears as failure, however, can be the very thing which leads us to what we are to do. Without failure we might stay where we are and never know the expansion that can be ours as unlimited consciousness. There are thousands of examples of men and women who apparently were failures, and yet out of those very failures grew the experiences that placed their names on the honor rolls of history.

To many persons failure is failure, and it is the end of the road. But is failure always failure? Is it not sometimes a stepping stone to something greater? If, at some particular moment, we are laboring under a sense of failure, we should not become despondent but rejoice, because most likely we are being prepared for the next step. If we can remember that there is a reason for our being here and that we have something to give the world, we will go from failure to success and step by step will be led to the work we are to do. In fact, in order to become aware of our purpose in life, we may have to experience such a rude awakening that we are shattered to the very roots of our being.

You and I, however, may be sufficiently receptive and responsive to the spiritual Impulse that we are awake to Its impartations and can find our place without some traumatic experience. When we know that the Spirit within is leading and guiding us, the robe

of Spirit envelops us and carries us to our ultimate purpose—
finding ourselves home in God.

Open Yourself to the Spiritual Impulse

No work, if done to the glory of God, is too unimportant or too
simple. Much as we may desire to rise in spiritual awareness and
become spiritual leaders or teachers, that may not be the special
purpose for which we were brought into the world. The unique
gift that we have to offer may be to create beauty for others in
music or art or to demonstrate the part that the spiritual qualities
of love, honesty, and generosity play in the success of a business
enterprise. There is no work or activity which cannot offer inspiration to others if it is based upon the understanding that it is being
poured forth from the Source. Infinity awaits every one of us if
we open ourselves to It, but until we do that, there is no way of
knowing what the divine plan is.

Many persons seeking to find their place in life think they can
sit down and do nothing, hoping that tomorrow something will
happen. To those I say: Begin where you are, be it ever so distaste-
ful, unpleasant, or humble, and do whatever you have to do to the
glory of God.

If you do your work with that attitude and your work does not
seem to reveal the glory of God, you will be moved to the place
where that infinite fulfillment can best be shown forth. Now is
the time to begin to release what you have to give. As you do that,
you will be led to what will be God's fulfillment as you, and it will
bring with it the reward and recompense. We have no way of
knowing what the ultimate fulfillment for us will be until we learn
to meditate and receive guidance and direction from within.

While active in my professional career, I meditated daily to
discover the divine plan for me, even while rejoicing in the work
given me to do. Then after months of meditation, a deep spiritual
experience came which brought with it the realization that I

should give up my career to devote myself to the teaching and practice of the principles of spiritual healing and living as given in The Infinite Way.

After that a most amazing thing happened. My goal had been to be the principal of a large school, but after I had given up that desire and had decided to change my work, the principalship in a nearby community, a position for which I had not applied, was offered me. After discussing this opportunity with my spiritual teacher, at his behest, I agreed to give up any attempt to reach a decision about the job and not even to think about it for a period of several days. At the end of that time I knew beyond all doubt what my decision would be.

Several weeks later another offer of a principalship came from another area, a better offer. Later, after I had turned in my resignation, a third one came, even better than the one before. Interestingly enough, these offers never came to me while I was seeking them and wanting them. As long as I desired and hoped and planned for that kind of a job, it eluded me. But when I released it, living out from the fulfillment within and having no thought of how that fulfillment would be expressed, the opportunities came thick and fast searching for me. In the years that have passed since then, there has never been a backward glance. It was an irrevocable step, but there has been no question about its rightness.

The principle set forth by this experience is that when a person stops desiring some particular thing and opens himself to the spiritual Impulse, It may find a greater work for him to do or It may make him more efficient right where he is. But whatever it is, he will be an effective instrument for God's activity.

Does this not really come down to the basic principle that if we want to change our life we must stop trying to change it outwardly? Because we are that divine Consciousness individualized, Its function is to show us the way we should go and to take us there step by step. Thus anchored in spiritual principles, we can look at our own experience and see how everything in our life has prepared us to reach the particular place where we now are.

There is an *I* within us that is come that we might have life and that we might have it more abundantly. Work should be a joyous experience, not a heartbreak, and so it becomes if we stop trying to have a purpose of our own and let the Spirit have Its way with us and fulfill Itself as us. Then we can cast every burden and every responsibility upon It, letting the government of our particular activity in life rest on Its shoulders.

It may appear that we are limited by certain outer factors such as our background, education, physique, and physical fitness, but the Spirit within knows neither obstacles nor barriers to Its activity. If our work is God's activity, it will be successful and fruitful, bringing reward and recognition, but if it is *our* activity it is always an iffy question. When it is a spiritual activity—and a spiritual activity can be driving a truck, sweeping a floor, or directing an orchestra—the Presence is performing it, and we become beholders watching It doing the work through us, although outwardly we are actively engaged in the work. Then we will never be concerned that the work given us to do is too great a burden. Infinity knows no limitation, and the work will be done, not by our wisdom or strength, but by Its wisdom and strength.

I *am come that My purpose in you may be fulfilled. Only stop having your own purpose. Let it be My purpose, for this is not your life: this is My life. I will take you by the hand, and I promise you that I will lead you step by step by a way that you know not of. Only be not afraid, for I am with you.*

You see only a small segment of your life, but I know its totality. Cast your burdens and responsibilities on Me, for My burden is light and My yoke is easy. Be still and know that I in the midst of you, I, the Spirit of God, am mighty.

If God is being fulfilled as our life and expressing Itself as us, can we not release every desire, every concern, and every fear? Does not God know how to fulfill Itself? In that recognition surrender is not difficult, because it is a surrender to our own divine Self.

The concept of surrender has carried with it such a dismal prospect that it has often been confused with the fatalistic attitude of resignation to whatever comes. Most persons are quite sure that what comes is not going to be good, especially if it comes from the dismal God they conceive of. But when we surrender to the will of God, that will is love, and love operates only in a way that brings forth good in ever greater degree.

Those who let God fulfill Itself as their experience discover how God reveals Its infinite capacity, which is not limited by a certain level of measured intelligence, a prescribed amount of education, or the environment in which one has grown up or now lives. As the infinite potentialities hidden within each person begin to emerge, he discovers his particular niche in life, the specific and unique purpose for which he is here.

"But," someone says, "look what I have to do: wash dishes, prepare the meals, do the shopping, and take care of all the humdrum business of daily life. Certainly that cannot be God's purpose." But how can anyone know? There is no work so menial that it cannot be done to the glory of God, and when it is thus done, the work itself becomes glorious.

If we are unhappy in the work that has fallen to our lot and think, "Oh, well, someday I'm going to have a more satisfactory job. Someday I won't have to do this kind of work. Someday!" What happens? Someday never comes.

Each day we have to live out from the standpoint of knowing that God is fulfilling Itself as us in every area of our experience. If we do that, not kicking against the pricks, not stewing and storming because we are not doing what we think we would like to do, but doing what we have to do with joy, then in due season we will be lifted out of that into work which is more suitable for us.

Many persons are unable to enjoy the present moment because they spend their time complaining about where they are and what they have to do. With that song going around in their heads, they never have an opportunity to be awake and aware of what God has prepared for them. They may be so stubborn that it takes a big shove to wake them up, and that shove can come in the form of failure. That is one way in which failure can become a blessing.

Every one of us must be willing to feel so inadequate that he opens the door for the divine adequacy to take over, that he may be the instrument for the Grace that was planted in him in the beginning.

What can happen very easily in days of sunshine when all goes well is that the subtle human tempter called the ego makes us think that we are pretty good and clever. Then we get our come-uppance or comedownance and discover that of ourselves we are nothing. We are something only in proportion as we open ourselves for the Spirit to flow through, and then whatever we do will be the Spirit doing it through us. All the credit, all the praise, and all the reward for our success belong to the Source. When we begin to take it unto ourselves is when we have to watch out to avoid a sad awakening.

Many times we are tempted to think how wonderful life would be if we could be doing what somebody else is doing. To seek to be like someone else is a denial of our own uniqueness. Instead let us always strive to be ourselves, do what there is for us to do, and be willing to work. All too frequently students have the feeling that when they embark upon the spiritual path, they are to do nothing but meditate all day long. There is no denying that meditation plays a significant role, but performing the duties at hand and keeping busy and active are also vitally important.

Business As a Spiritual Activity

Some persons who are unhappy in the situation in which they find themselves think that if they could only move some other place, find another job, or get rid of their employees and get better employees, all would be well. This is far from the truth. Whatever the problem, it has to be met within.

A dedicated and sincere student announced one day that she was so unhappy and dissatisfied with her work that she was quitting her job. My reply was, "That's all right as long as you are not quitting because of the job but rather because you have opened yourself to something better that has come to you. If you are still reacting to the situation and carrying it in your consciousness, however, it will follow you wherever you go. When you reach the point where you do not react to anyone or to any situation, then you are free and can go anywhere. It is all a matter of what is taking place in your consciousness, and you alone can be the judge of that."

She heeded the instruction, stayed where she was, and continued to work despite her longing to leave a situation not to her liking. She did more, however, than merely doing her work efficiently and effectively. During the course of each day she meditated for all those connected with the business, consciously praying for each one. She also prayed for the business, knowing that the business did not belong to any man but that it belonged to God.

It took considerable fortitude to persist in this practice, because many times she was being treated in a very unfair and unpleasant way. Nevertheless, she consistently and consciously kept the principles active in her consciousness until the day came when she was given her first increase in salary. Then another increase, and another, until she was recognized as the most important and valuable person in the whole business. Her employer realized that if she left, several accounts would automatically go with her because of the special quality of her work. Later, she was given extra help so that she was freed one day a week for Infinite Way work. Eventually she found herself engaged in a spiritual ministry.

How long did all this take? It happened over a period of years, but it was her blessing and her great opportunity because it forced her to live the spiritual principles she had been studying until they became a deep conviction. What an outstanding example this is of the part an employee plays and of his responsibility in the business where he works!

Humanly, an employee may think of his employer as grasping, selfish, and self-seeking, but he should realize that he is working for God, not for a person. God appears as the employer even though it may not look that way, and therefore the employer, thus recognized, can show forth only the qualities of fairness, honesty, reasonableness, truthfulness, and integrity, all of which stem from God. If an employee looks to his employer to be fair, he may look in vain. An employer of himself cannot be fair. Only God can be fair and only God can be just. As the spirit of God flows through an employer he will be able to express only fairness, honesty, justice, and reasonableness.

Business is not something grossly material but, seen in its correct and proper light, a spiritual activity. Every person should understand that the business in which he is engaged, if it is a legitimate and right activity, is not his business but God's, and that it is God's function to maintain and sustain His activity.

Every day a businessman should release his business to God and realize that whatever is necessary for its successful operation, whether capital, markets, or employees, is God's responsibility. The owner of a business, operating from spiritual principles, knows exactly what to do in every situation because he is an instrument for a wisdom far greater than any human wisdom, a wisdom that is the all-power which can provide whatever is required. Furthermore, it is the function of the employer who is grounded in spiritual principles to establish such a peace and sense of order in the business through his realization of oneness that there will be harmony in the particular operation. In the consciousness of oneness there are no longer employees and an employer. There is only One: one activity and one person, and that is *I*. *I* constitutes the employer, and *I* constitutes the employee.

An employer may think of his employees as indifferent, incapable, incompetent, and even dishonest, but no employer who is grounded in spiritual principles will expect his employees of themselves to be industrious or honest, because only God can be and only God can do. The employer must look to God at the center of his being. When he knows that God alone can be and do, then employees will appear who express those spiritual qualities of industry, honesty, and intelligence.

If employees seem to be incompetent, incapable, lazy, or stupid, this is an opportunity for the employer or the owner to put into practice the principle of impersonalization: that stupidity, ignorance, laziness, and other undesirable qualities are the carnal mind. They are never personal, because the only person in the activity or business is the divine Consciousness individualized, expressing infinite wisdom, energy, activity, and strength, all the capacities of the Father within, of that *I*.

Understanding the principle of one spiritual law operating, and applying that to the business, brings about the realization that the business, despite appearances, is not subject to the fluctuations of economic laws but is governed by spiritual law which maintains it according to a divine order. In omnipresent Spirit there can be no ups and downs.

Live As a Witness to the Divine Self in Operation

The spiritual life is not a withdrawal from the world, living separate and apart from outer activities. While it is beautiful and sometimes necessary to have periods of going away by ourselves, that is not the purpose, or end, of a life of Withinness. There will be periods of renewal and rest which may last for minutes, days, or even weeks. But always after the renewal or refueling, we must go back and play our part in the world so that the Self which we are may have Its instrument and find expression as us.

The life of Withinness brings us far greater activity than we could have hoped for, so much activity that we may cry out, "Oh, God, please, not quite so fast. Just give me a little time to catch up." But It doesn't. It keeps right on pouring forth and expressing because that is the nature of the infinite Self. And It always expresses Itself in an abundant, beautiful, and peaceful way.

The spiritual life is a mystical life of conscious oneness with God. In that conscious oneness everything we will ever need is already within our consciousness. Seeking the things of the world gives way to the wonder of discovering the glories of infinite Consciousness out of which flow the hidden treasures.

It is not that there are no problems as we go forward on our spiritual journey, but the problems cease to play a dominant role in our experience. It is the life within us that challenges our attention, a life completely independent of any person, any circumstance, and even independent of our body. Living out from that Withinness, the reason for being in this particular life experience is shown us, and we discover our purpose and function in life.

If God is to have expression as you and as me, we must be willing instruments, willing to listen and to be open to the way that God has chosen for us. Many times we experience trouble, pain, suffering, and sorrow because we are unwilling to be still and follow the inner direction. In fact, we may even be so presumptuous as to feel that the way we have in mind is much better, instead of realizing that God is infinite wisdom and that It has ways of bringing Itself to fulfillment that are far more beautiful and far greater than anything you or I could have imagined.

There are those who have turned to the Spirit and found that It has brought them by new and untried ways. It has led them into avenues of expression heretofore unknown to them. But the Spirit within knew that this was the way in which It could best be expressed.

God at the center of our being can accomplish whatever is necessary to be accomplished. If it is a new idea that must come forth, God at the center of our being will unfold as that idea. If it is mountains of work that must be accomplished in a limited space of time, whether household work or business activity, God at the center of our being can perform it more efficiently than we could, but only as we learn to listen and turn within for that inner guidance which is ever awaiting our recognition.

Each day should be an adventure, a new experience, because God is so infinite that It never has to repeat Itself. Just as every snowflake is different, so every moment in which God is living our life can be a new, vital, rich, and glorious experience, not the humdrum kind of repetitive life whose hallmark is dullness and boredom.

On the spiritual path there is never any dullness but only the adventure of each moment. It is like driving down a winding country road that we have never been on before and being amazed at the new things that are constantly coming into our view, moment by moment, as the car ambles along.

Our reason for living is that the infinite Consciousness which we are may find an outlet and expression. Within us is a Presence and a Power that is greater than anything in the world. Only a realization of this can give us true freedom from the burdens, the responsibilities, the struggle, and the strife of everyday living. Whenever we have the sense of being overburdened with the problems and the work of the world, let us stop and realize:

This is not my responsibility: this is the responsibility of the Consciousness which I am, the responsibility of the life-force of the Tree to which I am connected. That Consciousness is an infinite wisdom, and It knows how to perform and fulfill whatever It gives Itself to do as me.

When we learn to go within, that is, to turn away from outer activities and be silent, it will be as if that Consciousness within us is speaking and saying:

Come unto Me. Drop your burdens, and I will give you rest, rest in the midst of the most intense activity, for I, who have given you this work to do, will do it for you.
If it is business, I will do the work, and I will be there to provide

*whatever is necessary for Its success, whether it be capital, custom-
ers, or material. If it is housework, I will do it, and I will make
of your home a more beautiful place than you could have thought
of. I, the Consciousness that you are, will provide it for you. For
this is My work, not yours. This is My responsibility, not yours.*

Yes, there is that within us which knows exactly what is necessary, because the divine Self knows what It needs for Itself. It does
not know what we as human beings need, but It knows what It
needs, and it is Its good pleasure to provide it. So life becomes
a matter of being a witness, a witness to that divine Self within
us in operation, and we behold that which "eye hath not seen, nor
ear heard."

7

There Shall Not Be Room
Enough to Receive It

Bring ye all the tithes into the storehouse, that there
may be meat in mine house, and prove me now herewith,
saith the Lord of hosts, if I will not open you the
windows of heaven, and pour you out a blessing, that
there shall not be room enough to receive it.

Malachi 3:10

The concern many persons feel, as they measure their supply in
terms of diminishing bank accounts, a fluctuating stock market,
and rising inflation, can be alleviated only as dependence on such
material reliances is replaced by an understanding of the real
nature of supply.

Supply and security cannot be found in any of the externals we
see or touch. True, the *forms* supply takes are visible, but supply
itself can never be seen. And why not? Consciousness, invisible
Consciousness, is supply, and therefore supply is as invisible as
Consciousness is. Such a concept may be unacceptable to the
person steeped in a materialistic way of life and may be difficult
even for the seeker on the spiritual path to understand. After a
lifetime of looking to persons and things for the necessities and
pleasures of life, it is almost impossible for a person to accept the
truth that the Kingdom of Allness is within and that out of It
flows all good.

The authority for this principle is found in Scripture. Jesus fed
the multitudes, not out of anything outwardly visible, but out of
the infinity of that divine Consciousness which was his individual
consciousness. Out of that came the loaves and fishes.

Supply can never come from outside: supply is within. Supply
is our invisible consciousness, and that consciousness appears as

whatever our particular need may be: food, clothing, shelter, companionship, money, capital, business, or employment. The supply, however, is never in the food, in the money, or in anything that can be known through the physical senses. Supply is invisible Spirit, and that Spirit is more real than anything in or of the world. Everything that can be seen, heard, touched, smelled, or tasted fades, deteriorates, decays, and passes away, but not Consciousness.

If Consciousness is supply, where then is supply? Where, but omnipresent where we are? Is our consciousness some place where we are not? Can we be separated from our consciousness? And if our consciousness is our supply, can we be separated from our supply? How great is our supply? Is it not as great as our consciousness? And how great is that? Unlimited, infinite, including the whole universe! That is how infinite our supply is, too. If supply is omnipresent in our consciousness, then all we have to do to experience the infinity of supply is to release it.

Some students of metaphysics have been taught to make a list of what they want, to visualize it, and to try to draw it to themselves. Does that not violate the principle of supply? The infinity of supply is already within us. How can we draw to ourselves what is already ours? The only question is how we can let it pour out of us. How can we release the infinite consciousness which we are? Do not most of us think that in order for it to pour forth from us, we must have so many dollars?

When I first learned of and accepted this truth, I had to work my way through a very serious problem of supply which seemed almost insurmountable. At that time I was attending church regularly, and that seemed to be the place where I should begin to pour, but I didn't have an extra dollar to put into the collection plate. As I worked with the principle of supply, I saw clearly that the principle of giving, releasing, pouring, sharing, and letting go had to be acted out and lived. All I could think was: How can I share when there is nothing to pour?

Nevertheless, I was determined to center my attention not on what I did not have, but on what I did have. What did I have? Well, I had joy. Yes, I did: I had a joy that no man could take from me, so I could let that joy flow out. But I had something more than that. At that period in my life, I had a little time every Sunday afternoon during which I could write brief cheery notes to fifteen or twenty of my mother's contemporaries who were shut-ins, many of them isolated and very much alone. It was my way of releasing the only thing I had to give: a little bit of time and a great deal of joy and love.

It was not long before the principle of supply began to operate in a very surprising and interesting way. Every Monday morning my colleagues who rode to school with me noticed all the letters I was mailing. When they asked about them, my response was quite noncommittal, but soon gifts of all kinds of beautiful note paper began to be showered upon me. One friend who learned more about what I was doing even included stamps. The supply was already flowing back to me as the reflex action of the only thing I thought I had to give: a little time.

Often persons who have millions of dollars are still poor because they are afraid to release their wealth. They spend their time counting and hoarding their possessions. With their almost inexhaustible supply of the world's goods, they live pinched, narrow little lives, clutching at their millions. Are they happy? Are they fulfilled? Are they rich? How can they be when they do not know how to use what they have? Only as we use what we have with wisdom and intelligence do we really have it. Only what we give away is ours forever. Only that has real value.

On the other hand there are those whose bank account may be relatively small but who always have a sufficiency of supply. Whatever is given them to do, they can do it without concern because they have realized that their consciousness is supply, always omnipresent and available. They may not have thousands of dollars stored up, but whatever is needed is there, always: "Before they call, I will answer"—not afterward, but before.

Every person has something to give, and it is with that he must begin. Givingness has many forms. It may be a giving of food or outgrown clothing. It can be money or service. Sometimes it is just a smile or a flower, but when it is a gift of the Spirit, given out of love and sharing, it cannot help but bear fruit. The greatest gift of all can be a silent giving of our spiritual light to our friends, our neighbors, our enemies, and the whole world. What is important is that there be a givingness and a willingness to let Infinity flow out. Unless we do that, all the Infinity in the world will be of no value to us.

But if a person gives with the expectation that there will be some kind of a return, he has set a trap for himself. Giving must be done with no strings attached and with no desire to get anything from it. It must be prompted by love and by the realization that we are giving out of Infinity, and that Infinity cannot be kept bottled up in us. Eventually will come the great truth that all we ever have is what we give away.

Many times the very persons to whom we give the most may give nothing in return. That is not important. Then somebody to whom we have given nothing may suddenly pour out so much upon us that there is not room enough to receive it. Giving is important because it is acting out our conviction that supply is within our consciousness.

The Principle of Supply Illustrated

Four scriptural passages which contain the step-by-step unfoldment of the full and complete principle of supply have been of inestimable value in attaining the realization of the invisible, infinite, and omnipresent nature of supply, not only to me but to students with whom I have shared them.

A few years ago a man I had never heard of called from a distant city and told me he was in a precarious financial situation. He didn't know what he was going to do. He owed so much money that he was about to declare bankruptcy. His insurance business had come to a standstill. I explained that while there was nothing I could do to help him sell insurance, I could perhaps help him understand that, contrary to appearances, his real need was not to sell insurance but to gain an awareness of his true identity as consciousness and of the spiritual nature of supply, adding that what I was about to tell him was so simple that he might think it could not possibly be of any help. He assured me, however, that even though he might find it hard to accept, he would like to try.

"All right, let's take one thing at a time, and while you are doing this try, if you can, to forget about the apparent hopelessness of your situation." So he began with one simple principle with which I myself had worked and found very helpful: "The earth is the Lord's, and the fulness thereof." That does not sound like much comfort to a man who is about to lose everything. To his credit, however, when I gave him this first quotation, he did not arrogantly protest, "Oh, I know that! I've read it many times." Of course he had read that the earth is the Lord's, but he had the humility to recognize that reading something is far different from having the consciousness of it. Furthermore he was in such desperate straits that he was willing to do anything.

"Very well, then," I said, "every morning when you wake up remember that 'the earth is the Lord's, and the fulness thereof.' Now what does that mean to you? Does it not mean that everything you think of as yours belongs to God? You think you have a house; you think you have a wife; you think you have a child; you think you have furniture; and you think you have a depleted bank account. Give it all back to God, where it belongs. It never was yours. It always belonged to God because 'the earth is the Lord's, and the fulness thereof.' "

So he began to work with that and shortly thereafter wrote me a letter in which he never even mentioned the problem. Instead he wrote about what was coming to him in consciousness and how he was beginning to catch the principle.

Through his meditation on, and practice of, the earth-is-the-

Lord's principle over a period of time in which he inwardly relinquished all claims to what heretofore he had considered his possessions, he was ready to go on to the next step. With the humility born of surrender he could now accept the divine inheritance of allness: "Son, thou art ever with me, and all that I have is thine." It was as if the Father had spoken to him in these words: "Yes, it's all Mine, but it's all yours, too. You are My son, so it all belongs to you."

How inscrutable are the ways of God! As soon as we give back to God what we thought belonged to us, the Father hands it right back to us. And does He say, "You get five percent of it or a millionth part of it"? No, He says, "It's all yours because everything that belongs to Me belongs to you—all that *I* have." And what does God have? Cadillacs, houses, stocks and bonds? No, God has peace, love, joy, life, all the spiritual treasures. All these are ours as heir to the riches of the Spirit which appear in due time as whatever may be Its fulfillment for us.

After this student had contemplated and practiced the second passage for a couple of weeks, it was clear from another letter that he was ready to work with the third scriptural passage: "I have meat to eat that ye know not of." How many times during the course of a day do we say: "I don't have. I can't do this because I don't have the money. I don't have the intelligence or the strength"?

The principle is: I have meat to eat that the world knows not of. I *have* the meat that never perishes, never spoils, never disintegrates, never shrinks. I *have* the water of life; I *have* the bread of life; I *have* the manna that falls every day. I *have*.

I asked the student to contemplate what he had. He could instantly see that he did not have what he thought he wanted and needed, so in his meditation and practice he did not violate his intelligence by claiming that he had something he didn't have. As he continued to meditate, however, what he did have began to come to him. He had life. Life was a quality and an activity of his being, and he had it. He had Grace, the grace of

God that is an all-sufficiency. He had the peace that passes all understanding. That too was an *I have* for him.

Rarely in our correspondence or in our conversations on the telephone did he say anything about the problem. He did not dwell on it, nor did he complain, "What am I going to do? I have, but. . . ." Instead he continued to meditate on *I have;* he read everything in Infinite Way literature which would give him more light on the principle; he practiced it throughout the day, steadfastly refusing to accept the appearance of lack, while abiding in the spiritual qualities omnipresent in his consciousness.

Finally he was ready for the last scriptural passage, which had meant so much to me and which clinched it: "I am the bread of life." To clarify this point, I wrote to him: "Do you see the difference between the two statements, 'I have meat to eat that ye know not of' and 'I am the bread of life'? You might become separated from what you *have,* but you can never be separated from what you *are.* And you are the bread of life. You cannot get it: you already are it. It is within you because of your own *I*-amness. You can never see the bread of life because supply is the invisible Consciousness which you are and which I am. Therefore, you do not seek to draw it to you; you release it."

He worked with that principle for a considerable period of time and then a letter, with a check enclosed, came from him in which he said, "Thank you. I don't think I need any more help." It was a beautiful letter, indicating that he knew the important thing was not the *effect* of supply, but gaining the awareness of the spiritual nature of supply. Not a word did he write about the problem, just, "It's all right. I think I've caught it." I never knew to what extent the problem had been resolved until some months later my attention was called to an item in a local paper from that city naming him as one of three men who had each sold a million dollars' worth of insurance that year, making them members of the million-dollar club.

This illustrates the importance of being willing to take some simple principles and work with them, rather than saying, "I've read that. I know all about that." Instead he worked with them. And what happened? A consciousness came, a consciousness of supply.

In his last letter he wrote, "Pray that I never lose it." But how can he lose what has become a part of him unless someday the little ego should take hold of him and he might think he, of himself, was something? In that way he could lose what he had gained.

It is so easy for a person to fall into the negative habit of "I don't have." When we are thus tempted, we should leave out the "don't" and bring ourselves up short with just those two words, "I have." What do I have? I have spiritual riches. I have a sufficiency. I have the kingdom of God within me. What more could I want?

No One Should Attempt to Live Beyond His Attained Consciousness of Supply

Spirit knows nothing of material things. It can give us only Its own substance and qualities. Amazingly enough, however, when Spirit imparts Its allness to us, that allness is interpreted through the mind as the satisfying of our daily needs. We never attempt to circumvent our own intelligence and assume we have some material thing that quite obviously we do not have. We meet every sense of lack with our own I-have-ness. I have! I have! What do I have? I have the grace of God, and that is sufficient for every need.

I desire nothing and I need nothing, for I am fed with the bread of life. Can I ask for better nourishment? I am clothed with the garments of righteousness. Can I wear more beautiful raiment? I dwell in the mansions prepared for me in "the secret place of the most High." Can I have a more beautiful home?

When we know and realize that we are forever one with infinite supply, never again will we fear lack. If our human sense of supply should be dissipated or dissolved in some way, *I* within will build it up again. In three days *I* will build up the temple, not only the temple of our body, but the temple of our supply. Furthermore, *I* never becomes less than Infinity: *I* never shrinks.

If we think of supply as something outside ourselves, we will fail to understand and realize that supply is omnipresent. Supply is within us. When we stand on that, the forms of supply will reveal themselves to us, but these forms will in reality be our own consciousness externalizing, appearing, and revealing itself.

The principle of supply is so immutable that it never fails. Those who have realized it know that nothing can be added to them and nothing can be taken away. Infinity is the measure of their being. It is never necessary, then, to depend upon other persons. Whatever demands are made upon a person need cause him no concern, because consciousness is forever unfolding from the standpoint of Infinity. When he knows this principle, he becomes that point through which Infinity flows.

In the area of supply, as well as in the areas of health, relationships, and legal matters, a person must live out from his attained state of consciousness. If he tries to live out from merely an intellectual knowledge of the principle of supply, he may run into trouble. A person should not go out and buy a suit hoping that someday he is going to have the money with which to pay for it. Although it is legitimate to use a charge account as a convenience to purchase merchandise, charging things when a person feels quite incapable of ever being able to pay for them may be an indication of a blind faith, but it certainly is not an evidence of a consciousness of supply.

Furthermore, a person who continuously lives on borrowed money is not proving the principle of supply. In fact, a person who charges or borrows indiscriminately is putting the responsibility for payment on someone else: the department store, the credit man, the banker, or another person. A person with a consciousness of supply will have the money necessary to pay for whatever he purchases, and a charge account or loan will merely be utilizing the convenience of present-day business practices.

This is in no way a contradiction of Jesus' instruction to go "without purse and scrip." He was talking to his disciples, who had attained a state of consciousness that had realized the incorporeal nature of being which needs nothing of a material nature and is therefore not relying on material supply in any form. Persons who charge goods, not because it is a convenience, but rather because they do not have the money with which to pay for them and have no prospect of getting that money are still relying on money and on material forms of supply. But the person who lives out from his consciousness and knows that consciousness is infinite supply can go out on whatever his mission may be, and the money will always be forthcoming. It is an entirely different level of consciousness.

The principle of supply must be lived, and it cannot be lived if every action is a denial of it. How can we say, "I am the bread; I am infinity; I am all," and then seek to get something? Rather, our whole motive must be to distribute, to release what we have, and to give, letting the effects of supply flow out from our realized consciousness.

What do we have to give? We have God's grace, and that Grace is our sufficiency. You have it. I have it. Everyone has it. It must be expressed concretely, however, and not be allowed to remain in the realm of abstraction. Unless there is enough left over to share with those who do not know this principle, there is not really a sufficiency. Giving is an act.

Gratitude As a Facet of Supply

Gratitude is one of the most important facets of giving. Every time we say, "I thank Thee, Father. Let the gratitude which fills my consciousness for Thy unfailing love pour forth into this world to awaken those who do not see the need for it," we release this essential quality and, to the degree that gratitude is expressed, we *have*.

One little boy who had been taught by his mother to give thanks to God for all the good that came to him opened his eyes wide when a piece of delicious apple pie was set before him and gratefully exclaimed, "Oh, God, again!" Gratitude is part of the commitment to which every spiritual student must be dedicated.

Supply is basic to every human problem. It may not be a supply of money that is needed: it may be a supply of happiness, health, or purity. Whatever it is, it goes back to that one principle: I already am, and I must let what I am flow out from me. I must let it shine forth to all those who have not yet realized the truth that they, too, have the same Infinity within them and can never be separated from It.

With the consciousness of Infinity fully realized, abundance is assured. Strangely enough, abundance then no longer carries with it any great significance. In the material way of life we set store by things and feel that having them is all-important, but once we become detached from them, it makes little difference how much or how little we have. There is an inner realization that Infinity is ours as infinite Consciousness individualized.

What Are Our Priorities?

At some time in his ongoing every student discovers that whatever sacrifice he makes of time, money, or effort for the purpose of spiritual unfoldment returns to him, at first in full measure and later a thousandfold.

Some years ago my car, which I was driving in the curb lane, became the target of a head-on collision of two other cars traveling in the center lane. To my great dismay, my brand-new car was smashed and all those in it badly shaken up, although we were in excellent condition compared with the seriously injured passengers in the other two cars. I could hardly think about how my ankle hurt: all I could think about was my beautiful new car, now dented and twisted.

The police took me to the emergency room of a nearby hospital. After x-rays were taken I was told that while my ankle was not broken, the sprain was so severe that it would result in considerable suffering, and that to heal it would require me to be off my feet for several weeks.

When I was taken home, a call for spiritual help was immediately put in to my teacher, Joel Goldsmith. Later in the day the horror of it all overwhelmed me, and I found myself in a state of shock. Then, just as suddenly, I felt as if warm, tender arms were enfolding me as the awareness of the Presence engulfed me.

The next day I was able to walk with the aid of a cane and go to school. I realized that I must know more about spiritual healing principles, something I had shied away from because I was interested primarily in attaining conscious oneness with my Source. But, having experienced such a miraculous and practically instantaneous healing, I felt I must know more about how it had been accomplished. I was sure I could learn this by attending a class my teacher was to give on the west coast of Canada during the summer vacation.

The case in connection with the accident, however, had not yet been settled. With hundreds of dollars of damage to the car and many other expenses and obligations to be met, it did not seem sensible to go off for the summer to a class so far away. Nevertheless, although it would take practically the last dollar of my savings account to attend the class, I realized that I must go whether it made sense or not.

It did not look as if the case would be settled within any reasonable time, because two insurance companies were in conflict over which one was responsible for making compensation to those involved in the accident. Despite this complication I left for the class. After I returned my lawyer called me and said that he would have to take the case to court to recover damages. At my insistence, he unhappily agreed to wait before he took any further action.

The next day two insurance adjusters called on me for more complete details about the accident. I gave them an accurate account of what had happened and only later learned that these men represented the insurance company with which my lawyer was trying to reach a settlement. When he heard of the incident, he was not only indignant but he rather angrily said that I had certainly ruled out the possibility of getting any kind of a settlement.

That night I meditated for a long time. Even now I can recall the force with which the principle came through to me that there is only One: no plaintiff, no defendant, no judge, and no lawyers. There is only God appearing as each and every person involved. To the amazement of my lawyer, within two days a satisfactory settlement was offered by the insurance company.

Why have I related this incident? Because it bears out the point that no one whose motive is pure ever spends anything for spiritual unfoldment that does not come back to him. The amount of the settlement included exactly enough money to pay for all the damages and expenses incurred in the accident, and in addition enough almost to the penny to cover the cost of the trip to the class.

This is a concrete illustration of the truth that when the motive is right, anything given out or put forth in the search for truth returns in some form or other. It might not always be in such a clear, plain, and specific way as in this situation, but even then I realized that this experience and its resolution had been given to me, not for the moment, but so that it could be shared with others to show how the principle operates. Many people who profess to be seekers of truth are unwilling to sacrifice as much as the price of a book or the cost of attending a class, but they never hesitate to sacrifice everything they have for a new car. Plainly it is a matter of priority of values.

The principle of supply as embodied in our consciousness never fails if it is practiced to the point of realization. When, through meditation, our mind becomes sufficiently still to be a transparency for Consciousness to pour forth, supply will gush out in sufficiency.

The transformation may not come in a minute. It didn't with me. For a long time, whenever any money came in or I paid out a dollar, I had to remember that whatever came in or went out was not mine but God's. I was merely the custodian of it until it could be released or transferred to someone else. What good is a stagnant river? Only the river that is constantly flowing has fresh, clear water.

Shortly after I opened the first Infinite Way Study Center, while I was still active in my profession and also going to the Study Center several days and nights a week, it came to me after a deep spiritual experience that I should give up my lifetime career and devote myself to Infinite Way work. But where would the supply come from to provide for my needs? If I gave up my position, there would be no salary, no security, nothing on which to rely. Then the words of the prophet Job came to me, "He . . . hangeth the earth upon nothing."

So on the Fourth of July, a most appropriate and symbolic day, I dropped an envelope containing my resignation into the mailbox. I realized that I had taken an irrevocable step. I scarcely breathed as I stood there. No words came to me. I did not say, "I have" or "God is my supply" or "Supply is invisible and infinite." Those principles were so deeply embodied in my consciousness, because of the years of practice that had gone before, that now there was not a single thought, just nothing, absolutely nothing. For how long I do not know, perhaps just a few seconds, there I stood. A complete vacuum enveloped me. The whole world had been cut out from under my feet, and I had no way of knowing what the future would be. In that awesome moment I knew I was resting on No-thingness. But from that day on I have never had a concern or a worry about supply. All my needs have been provided for and always with twelve baskets full left over.

In that one second when there was no thought at all, only the deep silence of a total vacuum, the healing came. I was silent because there wasn't anything I could know. What was there to know? So I just stood there, right there at the mailbox on the corner. That was the healing of lack and limitation and the opening of the doors of Infinity for me. One moment of silence can do that—I mean absolute silence, not an induced silence where we sit struggling to become silent. This was a spontaneous silence which came as the fruitage of the meditation and the practice that had been going on for thirteen years.

Everyone can reach that moment in which there is absolute silence, nothing at all on which to rely, and thereby open the door for the Allness that is within to flow out into expression. That vacuum is essential, if only for a split second, in every healing. The disease and the lack that seem so stubborn dissolve in the vacuum of No-thingness. That mystical state of consciousness reveals that which no man can see but which is more real and more substantial than anything that can be laid up in a bank, put away, or hidden in an old shoe.

The Substance within which is our consciousness can pour Itself forth in a moment of silence. It can pour forth as the healing of disease, as the reestablishment of relationships, as safety, and as the restoration of all "the years that the locust hath eaten." It matters not what is lost; it matters not how desolate we may be or how alone. The Consciousness that we are is the resurrection and the life. We carry within us renewal and restoration, and because no one can reach into our individual consciousness, no one can take it from us. Yes, a person can reach our dollars and take them, but he cannot reach out and take our consciousness, for it is invisible. That invisibility is the substance of which the visible is made.

Whether it is a diseased body, deteriorating or disintegrating organs and functions to be restored, an empty pocketbook, or a dead relationship, the *I* that we are, this God at the center of our being, is its substance. That is the spiritual treasure which we lay up "where neither moth nor rust doth corrupt."

8

Greater Love Hath No Man

Greater love hath no man than this, that a man
lay down his life for his friends.

John 15:13

During World War II, the wife of an official of an Indonesian province was captured by the Japanese when they invaded that country. While incarcerated in a work camp, she became so exhausted and ill from the lack of adequate food and the hard physical labor demanded of her that one morning she was unable to appear at the lineup to answer the roll call. When the count of prisoners indicated she was missing, the commandant had her brought before him and placed in front of the group. He then took off his belt and raised it to strike her with the belt buckle in such a position that it would hit her in the face and in all probability kill her.

As he raised his arm slowly, she said that she knew such hate as she had never thought any person could know. But suddenly and unaccountably in the midst of that feeling of loathing, a tremendous sense of love swept over her, and she was able to look through what appeared to her as the most heinous evil possible to what she realized, in her innermost heart, was really there: the very presence of God, the Christ. Enfolded in the awareness of that Presence, she was lifted above the horror facing her.

The commandant stood transfixed with his belt in his upraised hand. Finally he dropped his hand, sent her back to her quarters, and asked an aide who she was. After that the guards watched her more carefully and gave her a little extra food which helped her to survive the ordeal of the prison camp experience. In that crisis, faced with what appeared as the cruelest of persons and imminent death, she was able to rise to such heights of consciousness that for her there was only the Christ present.

You and I probably will never have to face as difficult a situation as that. Day by day, however, we do encounter opportunities to become aware that those persons we meet are God appearing as individual being. Anyone who appears to us as a Pilate, possessing all power, is really the presence of God, and the only power he can have is the divine power which is a power of good and a power of love.

Personal Sense Is Dissolved in the Recognition of the One Self

As long as there are human beings with whom to deal, there will be someone with whom to struggle. What appears as a problem person, however, actually is a sense of a selfhood apart from God. But can there be a selfhood apart from God? Can there be any person other than the one divine Person? Is there room in Omnipresence for anything other than the One? One means one, and that One all-inclusive. There is only one Self. That one Self appears infinitely. Because of a false sense of separateness, however, a personal sense of that one Self has sprung up, and it is this personal sense which we identify as a person, good, bad, or indifferent. But it is not a person: it is only a false sense of the one Self, the one Person, of the *I* that we are.

What I am seeing as a person who is sick, dying, deceitful, or dishonest is personal sense, a false sense of a person. It is not your false sense and it is not my false sense. It is a universal personal sense which everyone has accepted through generations of human conditioning.

As long as we personalize, that is, look upon a person as good or evil, there will be someone to fear, someone to love, or someone to hate. Always there will be fear: the fear that those who love us will be removed and that those who hate us will not be removed.

All of us have had the experience of thinking that some person has done something of a harmful nature to us, only to find out later that it was nothing but our imagination, a picture we were entertaining in the human mind, which is always volleying between good and bad. We place fixed labels on persons: this person is so good, so wonderful—and he is, for a while! But sometimes the friend on whom we pinned such faith and hope becomes quite different, almost a complete reversal of the picture of him we had held in our mind, a concept—good, bad, or indifferent—which is never the truth about a person. One who might seem a paragon of virtue to some might be the most difficult, unpleasant person in the world to others. But the same person could hardly be both. Both are mental concepts of the person.

What a difference when we turn to the Center within and rise in consciousness! Then we are no longer looking at pictures of persons. Instead the Spirit within shows us the true nature of the person, and in meditation tells us that this is our Self, for there is no other than the one *I* within us. As we free ourselves from the personal or false sense of life, we awaken to the boundless freedom that comes when every person we meet is recognized as God individualized. Rather than judging, condemning, and criticizing, we accept nothing less than perfection.

This does not mean that evil actions are to be overlooked or that the person who is permitting himself to be used as an instrument for the carnal mind should be called God's perfect child. Many times strong action must be taken in dealing with such persons. But inwardly it must never be forgotten that evil acts are the carnal mind, a temptation, and always impersonal, to be recognized as a nothingness—personal sense, which has no person in whom, on whom, or through whom to operate.

When we rise to that level of consciousness where we are able to recognize the divinity of every individual, personal sense is dissolved. But personal sense cannot be dissolved in the person who is troubling us. It can be dissolved in only one place: within ourselves. There is no personal sense out in space. The hypnotism of personal sense lies in our misperception of the already spiritual and perfect identity of every person, an identity which is never lost. There is only one Person. There is only one *I*-dentity, but that *I*-dentity is individualized infinitely and that individual *I*-dentity always remains. As we lift up the *I* and see through the mists hiding from us the son of God in each and every person, we become truly loving.

Many years ago when I had occasion to ride the subway regularly, I saw the pain and suffering of humankind and at times the dregs of humanity. It was hard to look at such sordidness, sadness, and suffering, and not to react. Inwardly I found myself weeping. But one day as I looked at the saddest spectacle I had ever seen, like a flash it came to me: Why, back of that mask, *I* sit, *I*, the one and only *I*. How can I feel pity for that blessed *I*, beloved of the Father?

Never again did I feel that sadness, because back of the picture that was being presented, I could see in every person the Spirit of God. After that, as I recognized the *I* in persons, the tenseness often seemed to ease and a bit of lightness to creep in. Of course, there was no way of knowing if there was any response at all, but at least I maintained my spiritual integrity by seeing through the picture to the reality that was there. Through practice, I was learning the lesson my teacher had taught me, "Lorraine, inwardly you must be cold as steel to the appearance, but outwardly warm and loving, always expressing the compassion you feel."

Every student on the spiritual path must accept the responsibility of stripping off the mask that is on his own eyes—not on someone else's. He does not have to change anyone: what he has to do is to see through the mask which universal belief has placed over his eyes. With spiritual vision, we see God appearing where heretofore there had been a miserable or impossible human being.

We have all noticed those little reflectors that are placed a few feet apart on the highway to guide the motorist at night. No light shines out from them, but when an automobile throws its head-lights on them, they light up. So when we are able to see through the evil appearing as a person, impersonalize it, and lift up the *I* in him, we are the headlights casting a light on the unillumined disks of human consciousness, a light that is reflected back to us.

Love Is Seeing Through the Masks of Universal Belief

The world is starved for love, and yet the world does not understand the meaning of real love. It has never understood love. Is this not true of most of us? We look at what is evil and unpleasant in a person, pretending to love that, and end up by being complete hypocrites. It cannot be done. No one can love the evil; no one can love wickedness.

The way to love or forgive is to strip away the personal sense of Self and see God back of the appearance. It is well-nigh impossible to forgive many of the things we see, but we can forgive to the extent that we impersonalize and understand that what we are seeing is never a person.

If we believe someone is going to take something from us or do us an injury, we are living under the universal hypnotism of personal sense. The truth is that there is no person to do us harm, to be wicked, evil, cruel, deceitful, or lustful. God is the only person there is, and when we see God as individual being, such a love will flow out from us that it will lift up everyone within the sphere of our consciousness.

When we understand our own *I*-dentity, never will we look to anyone for anything, not even for love, because as long as we look to others for anything there cannot be pure love. Real love is possible only when we are anchored in our own Self-completeness. No one has anything we need, but everyone can be an instrument for the love of God. Our attention is no longer centered on what we can get from anyone or what anyone can give us, but on how much we can let the love within flow out from us.

The hardest place to begin is with our family, with those who are closest to us. But begin we must. How much easier it would be if each of us could experience the awakening of one man who said, "This morning as I came downstairs after a rather indifferent night, still half asleep, I passed a member of my household with a monosyllabic greeting. Suddenly I realized, 'This person is God is disguise,' and I became aware of what I had been missing." How much all of us have missed in our homes, families, and associations if we have failed to see each person as God appearing, as the son of God disguised, wearing the mask of universal belief!

What we need to do is to see through all the masks universal belief has placed on human beings to the divinity within. They may not be aware of their divinity, but we are. This will help to set them free. Most of all, we will free ourselves because what we hold in the bondage of condemnation and judgment binds us, too.

Somebody in our home has to be an instrument for love, and we have no right to expect another person to fulfill that function. We have to be the instrument through which love flows out and radiates to everyone in our household. They are all longing for it. Give it to them. And the light that is within them, the love that is within them, will begin to be released. It is all an activity of individual consciousness, seeing through the concepts and thereby expressing that love that is greater than any human being can have.

Those who have been touched by the Spirit have the love that is willing to lay down its concepts of another to see God appearing as him, sometimes greatly disguised, but still God made manifest. If you could have God dwelling in your household, how would you treat Him? If God could suddenly appear as a person, how gracious you would be! You would do everything you possibly could for God. You would wait on Him hand and foot and give Him the very best you have.

Treating the members of our household with the respect and love we would give God would transform the atmosphere of our home. It does not matter whether we receive respect or love: we give it. It does not matter whether we receive understanding or kindness: we give it and let the divine Consciousness bring forth the fruitage.

As we look at each member of our household, the demand upon us is to see only God, appearing as the beloved son in whom there is no fault. Those who try this will be surprised at what will happen as they steadfastly hold to this principle in the face of every suggestion presented to them. If there is any degree of receptivity in the person, he will be set free. But we are doing something even more important for us: we are setting ourselves free.

This is the household of God. In this household there is no husband, there is no wife, there are no children, no brothers and sisters, no aunts, no uncles, no nephews, no nieces, and no cousins. No one dwells in this household or enters it but the son of God. There is only God, God expressing as individual being in infinite ways but always God.

The one Consciousness is the consciousness of every person in this household. All the activity of communication and relation- ships is taking place within the one Consciousness, harmonious and complete. There are no misunderstandings, because One can- not misunderstand Itself. It is all One, the one Consciousness communicating, the one Consciousness hearing, the one Con- sciousness understanding.

Such a realization will do much to eliminate the frequent misunderstandings that can arise in any close family relationship. Neither you nor I have any way of knowing how the Spirit will function in a specific relationship, but when we bring the Spirit of God to bear on the situation, that Spirit makes all things right. The situation may have reached the point where it is hopeless and apparently there is no way out. Nevertheless, that is still the picture, the mental projection. Our function is to see through that picture by recognizing the spiritual identity of all persons con- cerned.

A blurred focus may reveal many persons with many minds, but when the focus is sharp, we realize that there is just One. Then harmony and a fulfilling relationship result because the relationship is that of oneness. Those who cannot respond to our realization are removed. We do not remove them: It does. We let the Spirit do what removing needs to be done and bring about any separation—or reconciliation—that is to be made. Love is not weak. Love is so strong that there is nothing it cannot do.

To love is to do unto others as we would have others do unto us. What greater gift can we give to anyone than to see through the mask to the Spirit of God in him and thereby raise up the son of God? That is love, and that must be the basis of all relationships. And when it is, there will be peace on earth! It will not begin with thousands of people: it will begin with us and with our families. Every person can begin to love, not only those he thinks are dear, loving, and worthwhile persons, but those he considers his enemies.

A New Approach to Forgiveness

If there is a disturbing person in our experience, our job is to get busy. Get busy where? On him? No, not on him because there is no such "he." The only "he" there is, is the son of God. Do we have to change the son of God, correct his disposition, or make him more generous or less miserly? Do we have to do anything to him? Or do we have to correct the suggestion within ourselves by recognizing the impersonal nature of whatever characteristic is appearing as a person? What we have to do is to work on ourselves and continue that work until we see that there could not possibly be any person such as the one we are accepting in our consciousness. When we realize that, we are free, not by trying to change another person, not even by trying to make peace with him, but by making peace with our Self, and our Self is he.

This lesson is one of the most difficult lessons to learn. How many times we have heard someone say, "But you don't understand what this person did to me!" When I explain this principle to a student, that is the answer I usually get: "But you don't understand!" But I do understand. I know how hard it is to practice the principle. I know how long and hard I had to work. I know how hard a student will have to work, but I also know how rewarding that work is.

Early in my experience in The Infinite Way, a grave injustice was done to me. It left me very angry, full of resentment, and with feelings that certainly were anything but feelings of love and forgiveness. Nevertheless, I knew that forgiveness could not be just a word in my mind. I knew I had to live it, but in the same breath I knew that in all honesty I could not love and that it was impossible for me to forgive.

I remembered that Joel Goldsmith had told me at one time how he was faced with a situation in which he simply could not find it in his heart to forgive or to love. But he was willing to release it to God and let God love through him. "That's great," I thought, "but I'm no Joel. I don't want God to forgive this person. I don't want him forgiven."

This situation set up in me a severe inner conflict. Eventually, after many days of struggle with myself, came the resolution of the conflict in these words: "Suppose this person should ask me for spiritual help? Suppose he were in intense pain, possibly dying, and he said, 'Lorraine, will you give me some help?' What would I do?" Yes, what would I do?

Of course there was only one thing I would or could do: help him. Therefore it came to me that every time I thought about this person, I would look upon it as a call from him for spiritual help. Every time he came into my mind I would respond as if he had actually called upon me for help. Instead of thinking what I really thought about him, which was anything but complimentary, I reminded myself that God constitutes individual being and that only the qualities and capacities of God can be expressed through and as an individual.

Not once a day, but as many as forty times a day and even more, as many times as the thought of him nagged and gnawed at my consciousness, I held to his spiritual identity. I recognized his Christhood. Over and over again, how many times I could never count, I realized that God constitutes individual being. It was not easy. It was hard, harder than anyone could ever know.

One student protested when I tried to teach her that the Christ is in everyone, "Well, I don't think the Christ has very good judgment." And I certainly felt at times that I could agree with her. So it was a discipline not to permit myself to think what I really thought about the person and situation, but to remember that God constitutes individual being and that only the qualities of God can show forth as any individual. The principle did not always come in those words, but that was the essence of it. The value of the practice was that it turned me away from thinking the critical thoughts that I wanted to think. And how I wanted to think them! How I longed to revel in the luxury of condemnation, hate, and judgment! But I forced myself to continue knowing that God constitutes individual being.

After weeks of continuous practice, it wasn't forty times a day that this man came to my mind, but a little less often, and after a couple of months my mind was filled less and less with resentment, anger, and condemnation. Sometimes a whole day would go by when he never entered my mind. But then there were times after I thought the problem had been completely resolved when it popped up again. So it continued, not for a day, not for a week, not for a month, but unbelievably for two solid years. Near the end of the second year, only rarely did I have a disturbing thought about the person, even though I had occasion to see him frequently. Finally the day came when there was no reaction, none whatsoever.

Since that time long, long ago, there have been many persons who have asked me for, and been given, spiritual help, but never in all the ensuing years have I given any person so much spiritual help as was given to this person. Never have I been so instant in season and so persistent. By all that is good and holy, he should have been able to walk on Lake Michigan at the height of the summer season. And what effect did all this help have on him? Did he change? I wish that I could say that he did, but he didn't, not in the slightest.

A mistake some of us who work spiritually make is to believe that if, through meditation, we are lifted high enough in consciousness, there will be a change in someone. When there is no change, we may feel disappointed and defeated and think that our meditations were useless. No, insofar as this man was concerned, nothing happened. But something did happen, and what happened was even better for me than if he had changed: I changed! Out of the whole experience grew a newfound freedom and an entirely different form of activity. I was lifted out of one situation and thrust into what was to become my lifework, all because I could not forgive a person, yet I knew I had to.

Let anyone who is working on a people problem take heart when he sees no change as a result of his work. Changing people is not our business. There is no one to be changed. The only change to be made is in our *concept* of what we see. All the work we do has to be upon ourselves, and the minute we reach out to heal a person, we are off the beam. If we have accepted a false concept, that is, if we have accepted anything less than the son of God, then the false concept in us must be corrected, and we are the ones who have to become free.

Real forgiveness is knowing there is no one to forgive. If we think there is, we have not even caught the meaning of forgiveness. No one can hurt or harm us when we know that God is the only presence and the only power. Established in that truth, we are aware that no one needs forgiveness.

If it is hard to forgive a person, we can meditate for him: know his real identity and the Source of his life. As the son of God, he is possessed of all the qualities of God and only God qualities.

"Love your enemies, . . . pray for them which despitefully use you." If we could begin, not by trying to love our so-called enemies, but begin by praying for them by knowing that they are God appearing and that God is being expressed as their consciousness, then love would flow out from us effortlessly.

If it is difficult for us to love some particular person, we forget about loving him. We begin instead to give him spiritual help by meditating for him, dropping the concept of him as a person, and knowing that since God is the only presence, God is the presence of this very person and there is nothing but God. If we could do that about twenty times a day for a week, a month, or a year, we would be so filled with love for the person that we wouldn't even have to try to love him: love would be overflowing.

Love Is Laying Down Our Concepts of Persons

It is not enough to talk about love. We have to love, and love is knowing the Christhood of every person. Of ourselves we do not have the capacity to love, but we can make of ourselves an instrument through which and as which God can love in us and as us. We may complain about someone, "He didn't even speak to me." Fiddlesticks! What difference does that make? We speak. "Well, he didn't do anything for me." We do for him. He may never appreciate it. Our good may be evilly spoken of, but that is not important. We do it. The Father, our own divine Consciousness that sees in secret, rewards us openly. We let God express His love and understanding through us.

When we are faced with inconsiderate, thoughtless, or evil persons, we might ask ourselves: Who told me he is a miserable creature? How do I know? Only with the mind. This is a picture in the mind. Now, mind, you be still; you be still and let God show me what really is. God, You reveal to me who this person is. You reveal to me the truth about him.

When God speaks to us, we will hear, "This is my beloved son in whom I find no fault." We will be satisfied when we see the son of God. Our work is to love by recognizing the Christhood of every individual we meet. When we do that, we walk this earth as a blessing.

No person can live for himself alone. Each one is his brother's keeper, and we fulfill this responsibility not by meddling in his affairs but by lifting up the divinity within him. This may have to be done thousands of times for the person we are trying to help. One attempt may not bring any results. It is like the dripping of water on the rock. Each drop of realization is wearing away the rock of human resistance, gradually breaking through the hard crust of separateness. There is no way of knowing which drop of recognition will dissolve that hard crust completely. But every time the *I* is recognized in a person, it helps to dissolve the crust of human selfhood with its selfishness and separateness. That can be our pouring forth, our giving.

Sometimes that outpouring may be given tangibly as actual bread or meat or water, but always behind that must be the spiritual giving and pure pouring. No one is laboring under such a deep sense of poverty that he cannot pour in that way. Let us pour, not to get, not so that it will come back to us, but pour because we have, pour out of the joy we feel because of our own Self-completeness. Of ourselves we cannot do this but out of our Christhood we can feed the hungry, heal the broken-hearted, and reform the sinner.

There will never be any love for us to experience, none whatsoever, except the love we ourselves express. If those who have little love in their lives would search themselves, they would soon see how little love they are expressing. When we express love spiritually love will flow back to us, not in a little trickle, but in such abundance that it will be like a great river of love flowing endlessly as the love we have expressed and are expressing. Love cannot come to us: love must be expressed.

The demand upon us is to love by lifting up the son of God in every person and above all not to forget to lift It up in ourselves, for we have been taught to love our neighbor as our Self. Perhaps one reason there is so much discord in the world, one reason there are so many ungodlike qualities such as hate, envy, jealousy, and unkindness, is because we have not yet learned to love our Self enough. If we really loved that Self we would love everybody, because we would see every person as our Self. When we attain that state of consciousness, it will be easy to let love flow out into the world.

The principle has been set forth. It needs only to be practiced. It cannot be talked about: it must be lived. Every temptation to accept twoness, two persons, must be met with the realization that God appears as individual being, with an absolute conviction that God alone is. As we impersonalize everything we see in this world of appearances, we will be given the discernment which will reveal the spiritual universe in all its wholeness and perfection. This is our function: to be a light embracing the whole world, including every person, in our consciousness of peace and love.

"Greater love hath no man than this, that a man lay down his life for his friends." I would like to paraphrase that in this way: "Greater love hath no man than that he lay down his concepts of his friends and enemies." We are all called upon to lay down our concepts of our neighbor, to sacrifice our personal sense of him, and to recognize his Christhood. That is the greater love, and that is the love we must give to everyone we meet: to see through the appearance and to recognize spiritual identity.

Are we not all somewhat like a crystal-clear mountain stream that has been covered over with debris? Are there not traces of the debris of personal sense still left in all of us? How much we would appreciate having someone push aside that debris and see beyond the pollution to the clear mountain stream that we really are! That is what love means. That is the gift we can give to every person.

9

The Armour of Light

The night is far spent, the day is at hand: let
us therefore cast off the works of darkness, and
let us put on the armour of light.

Romans 13:12

Good housekeepers usually plan to do a thorough housecleaning
at least once a year, preferably in the spring when all nature puts
on a new dress. During that spring cleaning, household items are
sorted, clothes and furniture no longer needed are given away, and
boxes of useless discards are tossed on the rubbish heap. Then,
after much scrubbing and cleaning, the house is put into ship-
shape order.

But what poor housekeepers most of us are with our lives! It
is not often that we have a really good cleaning out of our mind
and consciousness, not often. Seldom do we try to clear out the
clutter of false concepts and material beliefs that has collected in
our mind. In fact, just as we often discover in our domestic
housecleaning something we didn't even know was there, we
might find if we searched our mind that we have collected all sorts
of debris which stand in the way of our progress. We are usually
not even aware that we have let some unwanted world belief lodge
in our mind. A good mind-cleaning to clear the rubbish away
would be a rewarding activity for all of us.

How many of us are in the same state of consciousness today
that we were a week, a year, or ten years ago? Or have we left
behind much of what has previously bound us? To what extent
are we impersonalizing? How much freer are we of judgment?
Have one or two of the onion skins been peeled off so that less

of personal sense, that false sense of a person, remains? Have we inched forward even a little? Are we allowing great bundles of the past to remain in our mind and consciousness, permitting these to condition our present experience because of either their happy memories or their sad ones? We must be willing to let all that go.

Our spiritual housecleaning should release, surrender, and completely discard the past with its myriad mistakes. Are we really willing to give up those concepts that are cluttering our mind— the glories of the past, the past hurts and fears? Or are we going to cling to them, and think, "If, if. . . . If I'd only done that instead of this"? But just as living in the past must be given up, so the future also, with its hopes, desires, and fears, must be surrendered. Life cannot be lived tomorrow but only in this moment, not three minutes from now or an hour from now. If we are to live fully now, we cannot allow past regrets or triumphs or fear or hope for the future to remain in our consciousness and color our life.

As we look at ourselves from day to day we may not see any change, but if over a period of time surrender has not taken place, we have reason to be concerned. We cannot remain in a static state of consciousness: we either go forward or backward. Instead of taking one step forward and two backward and then two steps forward and one backward, our movement should be a steady, slow, gradual, yes, a tortoise-like progression if necessary, letting our consciousness be dedicated to the Spirit within so that It may take over our life.

To reach that goal, definite periods must be set aside during the day for meditation, study, and the practice of the principles. Not very much will happen if we do that for a day or a week, but if we do it every day without fail, we cannot possibly be the same person a year from now that we are today. Regardless of the amount or the degree of spiritual awareness and enlightenment we have attained, we have merely touched the surface of what lies ahead. How can anyone fathom Infinity? If we were to live hundreds of years and to work with the principles of spiritual living every day, we would still feel that we had touched barely the tip of an iceberg.

There must be day-to-day practice. Most important of all is the time given every morning to establishing ourselves in the consciousness of the one Presence and one Power which will guide us throughout our day, dissolving the seeming presence of any evil person or condition. Not only should this be done in the morning, but many times during the day we should bring to conscious remembrance the one Presence and the one Power.

Perhaps the greatest enemy to spiritual progress is inertia. We begin a program of this kind with great enthusiasm, with a sense of dedication and determination, and then if we are not awake and alert, inertia begins to take over. If we continue to live in the awareness of one Power, however, inertia will not find any place or activity in our consciousness, for our consciousness will be the pure, undefiled God-consciousness into which nothing of a disturbing nature can enter.

One way to prepare for the day is to read spiritual literature until a sentence or paragraph strikes us, something to spark our morning meditation, which we can carry with us throughout the day, think about, and meditate upon. We might begin with a statement such as "There is only one Presence." Out of that could come the realization that in that one Presence there cannot be the presence of many minds with conflicting purposes and interests.

Fill me this day with the consciousness of Thy presence. Let me realize Thy presence as the all and the only Presence. This day let me have no wishes or desires or will of my own. May I be receptive to Thy will that I may be an instrument on earth for Thee, responsive to Thy guidance and wisdom.

Of myself I do not have the wisdom or the strength or the power with which to go through this day and meet the demands that are made upon me. It is not my strength and it is not my wisdom: Thy understanding and Thy strength and Thy wisdom are infinite.

*These will carry me throughout the day so that it may be lived to
Thy glory.*

*In Thy presence there is no other presence to hurt, to injure, or
to harm. Cleanse and purify me from every belief that there can
be anything but Thy presence, which is the only Presence I meet
throughout the day, the presence of love, peace, and joy.*

We must establish ourselves every day in the consciousness of
oneness, beginning our day with the realization of the one Life,
the one Activity, and the one Law governing the entire day and
everyone in it, and we must continue to set aside moments of
awareness during the day when we take a listening attitude, waiting for that Presence to reveal Itself. In this way we will be
dwelling "in the secret place of the most High" and bearing
witness to the Spirit within, which is forever speaking and revealing Itself.

The Realization of One Power and One Presence
Is Our Protection

In the world we are faced with every kind of suggestion and
temptation. Destructive forces appear to be operating in the form
of bombs, germs, and malicious thoughts. Our daily work is not
to try to get some power to protect us from the evil, but to realize
that because there is only one Power and one Presence, there is
no evil from which to be protected.

*This day came into being as the operation of divine grace and
love, which govern the day. It is God's function to maintain this
day and everyone in it in the perfection that is already established.
Because of Omnipresence, there is nothing outside that divine
harmony, nothing to resist, nothing to be perfected or saved. The
one Presence is expressing Itself as the fullness of life and the
abundance of peace, joy, and all good. This is not my day, but
God's day.*

Today I stand in the presence of the one spiritual law which knows no opposites and no opposition. This law which I am maintains me every moment of the day and every moment of my life, governing my goings and my comings. It establishes me in the way, even though it may be a way that I know not of.

Today I go forward with confidence and assurance because my ways are ordered by divine Wisdom, and It directs my path and makes the way straight before me, smoothing over all the rough places.

Being an infinite, all-embracing Wisdom, It brings me the activity of this day and everything necessary for its completion. It knows what is necessary so that the divine Presence can be fulfilled in me, and It reveals Itself infinitely, abundantly, and perfectly.

Every moment of the day I live and move and have my being in the awareness that there are no powers to be overcome: no powers to fight, no powers to resist. There is only one Power, the invisible Consciousness which I am, from which I can never be separated. That one Power in which I abide is the power of love, resurrection, renewal, and restoration.

The peace that is beyond all understanding is with me as I walk through this day, living in the consciousness of the one Presence. In that Presence there is no room for the presence of discord, inharmony, disease, lack, dishonesty, or hate. There is room only for the presence of love, peace, life eternal, divine grace, spiritual indestructible substance.

In the realization of the one Presence my cup runneth over, because I am dwelling consciously in the presence of God, in the house of the Lord, where there is fulfillment.

It is we ourselves who determine and decide what our day will be. Every day is a blank sheet of paper upon which we write the record. Our day is not determined by persons, circumstances, or conditions. But if we let our mind become cluttered with the suggestions, seen and unseen, which we pick up, if we believe that we are victims of whatever is floating around in the atmosphere, so it is with us. If instead we recognize that we have inherent within us God-given dominion over our experience, we can face each new day with courage and conviction.

Does that mean that we have dominion over persons, or that we can walk up and down the world dictating to other people? No, not at all, and yet we do have dominion. The dominion lies in our response to what is presented to us. If we go out into the world filled with the belief that there is a power of good or evil outside ourselves that can act upon us, we may experience good or we may experience evil. But, if we realize that there is no power from without that can act upon us for either good or evil because all power is in the divine Consciousness individualized as us, we will not be blown about by the world belief in good and evil. If we respond by remembering that there is only one Power, one Presence, and one Wisdom, we are carried through the day peacefully and harmoniously.

I awake in joy to this new day which I have never seen before. I have no idea what the day holds for me, but if I am established in the consciousness of God, whatever it is will be an unfoldment of God's presence and activity. I stand as a witness to God in action in my body, maintaining the order and wholeness even of its inward parts; God in action in my home, bringing peace, harmony, and abundance; God in action in my business, governing it with infinite wisdom and intelligence; God in action in my relationships, establishing them in love and perfect understanding.

I recognize the limitless nature of Consciousness expressing Itself as my individual consciousness, and that Consciousness knows no barrier or limitation. I live only this day, and in this day nothing from the past can operate as cause or law upon the infinite Consciousness which I am. There can be no fear of the future, because God is always functioning. The one Cause is forever in operation, and, therefore, this day is a continuous unfoldment of the activity of the grace and love of the one Presence. The limitless nature of the Consciousness that I am reveals Itself as the Grace which is my sufficiency and which needs nothing whatsoever, but is complete and full.

This day I realize that I am not acted upon by outside powers because I am established in Omnipotence, the All-power in which there are no other powers. There is no power from without that can act upon me. All power flows out from the center of my consciousness.

The divine Wisdom which is ever present maintains me in my rightful place in the kingdom of God. I live in the world but not of it. Today, even while about the work of the world, I live consciously in My kingdom, where all is peace and where there is only fulfillment.

I am a beholder of God in action, God as the activity of my body, for this body could not move or function except for the Life-force that is within it. I bear witness to God as the activity of what appears as my concept of the organs of the body, which are governed by spiritual law.

This day I am not the victim of false appetites in any form because I am one with the Father, and in my oneness with the Father I am Self-complete. I need nothing external for my completeness or satisfaction. Completeness is a quality inherent in my being. It flows forth from within me, never dependent on anything outside my consciousness.

I take possession of my mind, for my mind is an instrument of God, and only the thoughts that God gives me to think can operate in, and through, and as my mind. My mind is not a battleground for universal beliefs and universal suggestions which testify to disease, lack, false appetites, unhappiness, or accident. Nothing can enter my mind that "defileth . . . or maketh a lie." My mind is the temple of God, and I keep it holy, sanctified for God's purpose, a clear transparency for the divine activity which is forever in operation.

I release my body to the divine government as I let loose all concepts about the body. In the silence and stillness I become aware that my body is the temple of God, a holy place formed of spiritual substance and maintained by spiritual law. Its function is to be an instrument for the divine perfection and to show forth the glory of God and the beauty of wholeness.

I release my home, my family, and my loved ones to the divine government. My home is the temple of God, God-governed, God-maintained, and God-supplied. All those in this home are of the household of God, showing forth divine grace. They are not my family but the family of God, each one a branch of the Tree of Life, maintained by divine Wisdom.

I release this nation to the government of God, knowing that in spite of appearances there is a divine activity in operation.

Today I live as a beholder. I am never the doer: I am the be-er, a witness to God-being as me, God-being as everyone I meet. Only love can flow out from every person as God-being, and every person I meet is gifted with the power of love and love alone.

Those who devote the first few minutes of every morning to this practice will eventually live in the security of God-realization. This morning work must not be a rigmarole, rattled off so fast that we lose our breath repeating it as we jump out of bed, rushing to make preparations for the day. It should not be approached with the feeling: Now I have to sit down and do this thing and I had better do it, or else. Instead we gladly give the first ten minutes, fifteen minutes, or whatever time is available to the realization of, contemplation of, and communion with the Presence within.

Becoming Aware of the Divine Government in Operation

During the day decisions will have to be made. Then is the time to remember that Omniscience knows far better than we do what the decision should be. If we have established ourselves in the consciousness of Omniscience, the direction in which we should go will be given us at the moment it is needed. The one trouble is that we want to know what to do a month or a year in advance, and that is not always possible. We must be willing to wait until we feel the stir of Omniscience within and are aware of It. Then when we have consciously established ourselves in It we can go forth with courage, conviction, and confidence, knowing that He within us, omnipotent, omniscient, and omnipresent, goes before us every step of the way and remains behind as a blessing.

The Presence provides the activity of the day and performs it without struggle, fear, or concern. There is a struggle only when we hop into the driver's seat and think we know how the day should go. This we do because we have not learned to trust divine Wisdom, which knows what we need. These needs are never material, but when we have the consciousness of the Spirit of God within us, we have the substance of which everything is made. All we need is that Spirit, and having that, we can be satisfied and be at peace.

Probably our biggest trouble is that we still think that God may fail us and not keep His promises. But God is always about His business of being God, and our responsibility is to release ourselves to Him.

Although there may be confusion in the world this very day and I may find myself in the midst of turmoil, I turn to that Center within so that It may dissolve the turmoil in Its peace.

I take our whole nation into that consciousness of peace so that it may experience peace in the midst of confusion, differing opinions, corruption, and disruption. "My peace" I give unto this land, not the peace of the world, but that spiritual peace which knows that the lust and the greed for power are not power. There is only one Power, that Power which flows out to light the darkness of human consciousness.

I embrace the whole world in this consciousness of peace so that it may know a true and lasting peace in which there shall be war no longer. There is no one with whom to contend or fight, for every person is that divine Presence expressing Its fulfillment. Each nation is Self-complete, never needing to strive with another to obtain anything but rather seeking to give and to share. I see all this world embraced in that peace which knows that human con-

sciousness is the only enemy and that human consciousness dissolves in spiritual consciousness.

Open Thou mine eyes that I may see truly and behold the world as it really is. Then I shall be satisfied, for I shall see that where confusion, chaos, and disorder appear to be, there is the very presence of God. Where lack, poverty, and starvation are, there is the infinite abundance of Spirit. Open my eyes that I may see that the government is on His shoulders, the government of my individual life, of this nation, and of this world. Under that divine government there is a spiritual law of order, peace, and harmony in operation, so that men can walk up and down the world without fear or concern. They do not walk alone, for the Presence realized is everywhere present and everywhere active.

I cover the earth with the deep silence that comes from resting in the consciousness of oneness, so the distrust, dishonesty, and fear which plague individuals and nations may be banished forever. Clad in that invisible cloak of silence, I cannot be touched by the weapons of this world, for I live not by might or by power but by the Spirit which knows no power. That silence is my refuge, and the everlasting Arms carry me upward and forward.

Those who have a deep enough awareness of Omniscience, Omnipotence, and Omnipresence must eventually awaken the rest of the world out of its deep slumber so that there is no longer striving and struggling, corruption, dishonesty, and lack of integrity in public affairs. No matter what the appearance, how difficult or how insuperable the problem may seem to be, there is a divine activity in operation.

Bearing Witness to the Glory of God

The Presence within is mightier than any claim to power in the world. It is greater than any problem and, being divine Wisdom, knows how to deal with every situation. Established in the awareness of Its ceaseless activity we walk with courage, confidence, and assurance, not letting the snares along the path entrap us or take from us our high purpose, which is to live this day that God may be glorified.

And what is meant by glorifying God? A little girl in Sunday school answered that question in this way, "I think we glorify God by living each day so that God will be glad that we are alive." Why could we not all go through the day, feeling that everything we do is for the glory of God, that God will be glad that we are living as His beloved son?

Perhaps it may come to you as it has to me so many times, "And the earth shall be filled with the glory of God," the glory that fills every nook and cranny of Its own spiritual universe.

This is God's day in which God is to be glorified in that I bear rich fruit. God is not glorified in my suffering or discontent. God is glorified in the joy, the gladness of heart, and the peace I carry with me throughout the day.

I live out from my God-given dominion, a dominion over the concepts that in my unillumined state I accepted. Now as the light within takes over more and more, the concepts fall away and the spiritual universe is revealed.

Let me have the discernment to see through all the disguises that appear as persons, recognizing that each and every person is empowered with Thy love, Thy grace, Thy truth, and Thy wisdom, and that each and every person on this earth is under Thy law.

In that awakened state I see everybody as the one Self expressing Its qualities. So I go out into the activity of this day clad in the impregnable armour of oneness.

The proper attitude for our morning preparatory work is one of silence and listening. Too many times, however, it is not possible to attain that state of silence because the suggestions, temptations, and problems of the world rush in upon us. Nature abhors a vacuum, and when we sit in meditation with nothing active in consciousness, something is bound to rush in. If we are not well-grounded in the truth of oneness, that something can be all the suggestions of the world that so easily find lodgment in our consciousness. Instead of dwelling on God and the things of God, we may let world suggestions engulf us as we sing our song with its sour notes over and over again.

Many persons misunderstand this morning work and think that its purpose is to make the mind a blank. Rather the meditation should be an activity of consciousness in which, to begin with, we use a contemplative form of meditation, consciously dwelling on the truth of God's presence, God's power, God's grace, and God's love. In fact, we are consciously realizing all the truth we know about the presence, the power, and the activity of the Spirit within us.

Living Under the Government of God

We are either opening ourselves to the one Consciousness and the one Presence or we are opening ourselves to whatever is floating around in the atmosphere, hitting one person in one way and another in some other way.

Each day our practice should begin by realizing the one Presence, one Power, one Activity, one Law, one Substance, one Consciousness. We do not rest and feel that it is complete, however, until we come to an end of contemplation and there is a sense of quiet and peace. It may be of much less duration than a second, so short that it is almost imperceptible. At first we are freeing the mind of its concepts by feeding it with truth, thereby establishing it in the consciousness of oneness. We have the power either to do what we will with the mind or to let the world do with it what it will. If we do not take conscious possession of our mind, our experience is subject to the world's ebb and flow —good at times and bad at other times.

The government of this day is upon His shoulders, so I will be glad and rejoice. The government of this life, which is really God's life, is His responsibility to maintain.

The government of this body is upon His shoulders. I release it to that which formed it of Its own divine Consciousness and which maintains the body in perfect balance with balanced activity. The spiritual substance of Consciousness, of which the body is formed, always shows forth the fullness of life, knowing no disintegration, deterioration, or degeneration. It knows no such thing as age, for I am as young and fresh as each new day with all the wisdom and intelligence of the eternal, everlasting Father. This day I release the body to the rhythmic activity of Spirit which maintains every activity of the body according to a divine law of harmony.

Since the government of this day is upon His shoulders, I release my home and family to the government of love, which maintains my home in a loving and peaceful atmosphere where beauty and harmony reign because God is governing and maintaining this home. I release every member of my family to the divine government, for each one is maintained by the Life-force, not by me. The Life-force which is flowing through every person maintains every member of this family, which in reality is not my family but the family of God. Just as I have no life of my own, so I have no family of my own. What I think of as my family is God's family, and God maintains His own family.

I release my business to the divine government, knowing that it is not my business but God's business, an activity of the divine Consciousness. Omniscience provides for this business and everything that is necessary to maintain its full and complete activity. Because this business is under the government of God, it is not subject to human laws or beliefs of economics. It is subject only to the divine government.

Today I go forth clothed in the armour of light, safe and secure. I do not live in the world, but I dwell in "the secret place of the most High," and nothing can penetrate, disturb, or harm that secret place.

The government of my mind is upon His shoulders, for this mind that I call mine is His instrument, open and receptive to God's thoughts and closed to world beliefs and suggestions. My mind is a transparency through which the divine activity is revealed.

I carry with me an atmosphere of peace which is impervious to the turmoil and discords of this world. As they hit against the Christ-peace, they bounce away.

Around me are the everlasting arms of Love. I nestle back in them and feel their tender support and care. With those Arms around me, there is nothing out in the world that can touch me or disturb the peace I feel.

This day I walk up and down the world as a blessing, recognizing the peace of God at the center of every person and carrying that peace with me wherever I go.

The government of this day is on His shoulders, and of His government and peace there shall be no end. The increase of His government and peace shall go on and on until our nation and the whole world enter into that consciousness of oneness.

How we awaken to the day should be a matter of concern, because many times the attitude with which we awaken will be the keynote of the entire day. Do we rise in the morning bogged down with the problems with which we went to sleep, or tried to go to sleep, letting them race around in our mind? Is our mind filled with concern and fear for the day ahead? Do we let the problems, frustrations, and difficulties of life push in upon us? It is hard not to have this happen and hard not to take the attitude of many persons who wake up each day of their lives with "Oh, God, another day!" And the tone of voice implies that it is not going to be a very good one.

Instead we should awaken with joyous anticipation at the opportunity to be a witness to the activity of God: "O God, another day in which to bear witness to Your glory! Another day in which to give my first fruits to You!"

If we do that, we are fulfilling the scriptural promise: "Bring ye all the tithes into the storehouse, that there may be meat in mine house, and prove me now herewith, saith the Lord of hosts, if I will not open you the windows of heaven, and pour you out a blessing, that there shall not be room enough to receive it." One of the most important tithes we can make is the tithing of our time, the giving of its first fruits to God. When that is our first concern, the blessings of the divine Consciousness pour down upon us and we are guided, directed, renewed, and restored throughout the day, proving that "they that wait upon the Lord shall renew their strength; they shall mount up with wings as eagles; they shall run, and not be weary; and they shall walk, and not faint."

10

Why Should the Work Cease?

And I sent messengers unto them, saying, I am
doing a great work, so that I cannot come down:
why should the work cease, whilst I leave it,
and come down to you?

Nehemiah 6:3

The alchemists of the Middle Ages labored to find a process by
which base metals could be turned into gold. They were never
successful, for they were working with inanimate and unrespon-
sive material. If we are able to change our limited concepts of
ourselves and the world we live in by a growing understanding and
awareness of the power, beauty, intelligence, and reality of the
spiritual world which surrounds us, we will have found the alchemy which transforms our world. Our tools are the spiritual
principles we follow, and our reward will be the gold we find on
reaching our goal: our abiding place in the temple of God and our
oneness with the Father.

Someday every person will awaken to find himself home in
God, and that includes all the persons who have never heard of
a spiritual teaching, who have no interest in one, and whose life
is totally devoted to pleasure. Many persons may have to spend
lifetimes before they awaken, and their journey may be slow as
they wander down enticing bypaths. Others, however, are unwilling to devote one parenthesis after another to their emergence
into spiritual consciousness. Having glimpsed the possibility of
awakening here and now, they seek to encompass the whole
journey in one lifetime. They have realized that whatever conceals
and perpetuates the masquerade of humanhood—the false per-

sonal sense of self—and keeps them from recognizing their divine selfhood must be cast aside, along with every concept and every human quality they have.

Just as the experienced mountain climber does not start out laden with too many burdens, so we cannot go forward on the Path weighted down with concepts accumulated over lifetimes. All of these burdensome concepts constitute the ego man, who has a self to be preserved, to be catered to, to be loved, and to be feared. Every burden which would retard our ongoing must be discarded if we are to make progress and maintain the spiritual balance required on the Path.

By now it must be clear that the dependencies and reliances to be surrendered are but the distorted pictures of an eternal perfection and wholeness. The demand is to surrender only the shadows, in order that we may live in the eternal reality of the spiritual kingdom. Most of the time we live in the shadow world, catching glimpses only now and then of the spiritual universe. But more and more our vision widens until one day we discover that we have been there all the time.

The way is to walk with a single-pointed vision, keeping our eye on the goal of conscious union with the Source. We carry our attained state of consciousness with us wherever we go, even into the next parenthesis, just as we carried with us into this parenthesis our present state of consciousness which brought us our particular home, environment, parents, and friends. We have now set our foot on the road to awareness and in so doing have said to ourselves: "I do not want to take the slow, tortuous path of evolution. I want to telescope all the parentheses to come into this one parenthesis, so that when I leave this parenthesis I move into the circle of eternity where there are no more parentheses, unless I so choose."*

*For a complete discussion of this subject, see Joel S. Goldsmith, *A Parenthesis in Eternity* (New York: Harper & Row, 1963).

With One-Pointedness, the New Consciousness Is Built

Every effort we make, small or big, is possible only because the grace of God has touched us and is pushing us forward. Through the grace of the single eye, with one-pointedness we build the new consciousness: the new heaven and the new earth.

The one-pointedness of Nehemiah enabled him to rebuild the wall around Jerusalem in spite of the diversionary tactics used against him. Sanballat, representing the hypnotic beliefs and suggestions of this world of twoness, presented one argument after another to convince Nehemiah to stop the work and come down to him. Nehemiah's response was: "I am doing a great work, so that I cannot come down: why should the work cease, whilst I leave it, and come down to you?"

So, too, with us. We are doing a great work, the greatest work of all, not building a material wall but building the wall of the new consciousness. Will we let the Sanballats of inertia, twoness, and separateness divert us from our purpose? Or will we heed the knocking of the *I* within and stand immovable on the rock of spiritual consciousness?

If at times building the new consciousness seems to be a struggle, it is because we resist giving up the visible for the invisible No-thingness that cannot be seen with the eyes. When there is nothing, no thing in the outer world to which we can turn, no one on whom to rely, no person to trust, when there is just nothing, we begin to discover that which we are. Because we are no thing, we are beyond all things.

In a moment of quietness how expansive, how great, is our awareness! This expanding awareness is our Self revealing Its many facets, the Self which is all-wisdom, all-knowledge, all-truth. All the knowledge, all the wisdom, and all the intelligence and capacity of the *I* are the knowledge, wisdom, and capacity of this Self, this Consciousness which I am.

Because I am one with the divine Consciousness, I am infinite, knowing no limitations, no boundaries, but everywhere present. This Self that I am is never touched by anything in the world or even by what happens to this physical sense of body. The Self is from everlasting to everlasting, knowing no beginning and no ending, eternally shining. As the veils hiding its brightness are stripped aside, Its light is revealed to the whole world.

That No-thingness, pure Spirit, can translate Itself into this world's experience in a far more beautiful way than anything we could imagine. It has no limits except those we place on It by becoming weary or by vacillating in our resolution. If we faint, if we falter, what we have attained can be lost for a time—not forever, only for a time. This house of awareness that we have been erecting may be battered by the wind, but it will stand. In the storm that clouds the attainment, the house may seem to have vanished, but when the storm is over it will be found to be just as solid and firm as ever.

There is a choice. We can decide how fast or how slowly we will go toward our goal of conscious oneness with God. We have reached the place of decision because now we know that there is no power from without that can act upon us, for all power is within.

The Divine Alchemy

And now, O Father, glorify thou me with thine own self with
the glory which I had with thee before the world was.

John 17:5

Does not the alchemy of awareness reveal the inner glory which is always present, albeit so well hidden that no one suspects it is there, least of all ourselves? The peace, love, and joy the Father planted in us in the beginning, before there ever was a material sense of world, is the glory no man can take from us once we have realized our oneness with the divine Consciousness.

The possibility of our transformation from the human sense of self to the divine Self permeates Scripture, which is really an account of a divine alchemy. That alchemy, through awareness, transmutes and transforms human consciousness.

The Bible calls it being born again, that is, being born into a new consciousness, a new dimension. It is not that something new, a new self or a new being, is to be brought forth; rather the clouds are to be dissolved that are hiding what is shining there within, probably begging to be recognized. Transformation of consciousness is impossible unless we are willing to let go of old concepts, let go of all the misconceptions held on to for so long, let go of those extraneous bits of humanhood concealing the eternal light which was ours from the beginning. As we go forward on the Path it seems as if the light grows brighter, but it doesn't. It has always been there in its fullness, revealed now to our expanded awareness.

The spiritual journey begins with the word God and ends with the word *I*. First we become aware of Something strong and powerful around us which gives us a sense of security. Before the end of the journey, however, we come to realize that there is only *I*, the Self. That is the journey we take: going from some power external to ourselves to the realization of that *I* within us which is freedom, for where that *I* is there is no bondage. The more we dwell on the spiritual nature of our being as *I*, the more we "die" to the human consciousness and the more we awaken to the Spirit within.

How soon the consciousness of that Spirit within, that *I*, will be attained depends upon how much we want it and how willing we are to face the challenges along the way. If we are courageous enough to keep our vision on the goal, we will not be among those faint-hearted ones who complain, "But I didn't think I would have all these problems." The problems come, but rather than being submerged by them, we rise out of them as the alchemy of awareness transforms our consciousness.

The Grace that brought us to this Path will take us all the way, but our progress depends upon our opening ourselves to God's dedication and letting that carry us forward. How much time each day are we willing to spend on transforming our life? Out of the depths of our gratitude, are we willing to give the first fruits of our time to God? Do we begin our day consciously abiding in the Presence, knowing that there are no powers to oppose that one Presence, and that therefore no weapons can be formed against us because there is nothing other than the One? Are we willing to establish ourselves in the consciousness of oneness every morning and then reestablish ourselves in it many times during the day? In this way we are in the world but not of it, moving in and out, but always carrying with us the consciousness of the one Presence and the realization that there are no powers outside that can act upon us for good or for evil, because all power flows out from the Center of our being.

The spiritual way of life is a way of living ever more effectively in the world and yet never quite being a part of it. We become so adept at keeping hidden that inner Something we have discovered that nobody suspects what is going on inside of us. We look like almost everyone else and we act like everyone else—almost. And yet there is a difference because we have discovered that we have within us the Source of life and the secret of all good.

If we could withdraw from the world, would we make as much progress? Would we gain as much awareness as we do living in the world, where we are constantly faced with challenges in the form of problems? Do not these challenges take us deeper than we would go if we lived as hermits? A hermit thinks he has escaped from people, but when he goes back into the world, people are still there and all the problems they present. On the contrary, when we go into the world we meet with problems involving persons until we reach that stage of consciousness where we have no persons with whom to deal but have only that blessed *I*, that beloved *I*, which we recognize in everyone we meet. That is living in the world but not being of it; that is "dying" to human consciousness and being "born" into spiritual consciousness.

Every time we "die" to some measure of human consciousness, we are born again. To be born again is an activity of consciousness that comes from within and is not brought about by any ceremony or ritual. To be born again is to see the whole world new, heaven here on earth, the spiritual universe which this earth is. The born-again experience is the awakening to a new state of consciousness.

With the new birth, the new awareness, comes a transition to the point where we of ourselves are no longer being good, kind, or loving, because we have attained the humility which knows it is the Spirit of God in us that acts and is the doer. *I* within can do all things, and the sense of the little "I" withers away so that the *I* that we are may come forth in the glory we had "before the world was."

"Before the world was," everything was a state of *is;* not becoming, but *Being.* In that state there is nothing to attain, nothing to achieve. We are living out from our own divine Beingness, and that Being within us, that Spirit, that *I,* is the doer which performs the work we are given to do. Our body and our mind are merely the instruments of that *I.*

No longer is there concern about the fruitage. Our only concern is to be an instrument of God. Then It uses us for Its purpose. We are simply witnesses, beholders of It operating in us, through us, and as us. But It is doing the work, not we ourselves, so whatever is accomplished, the glory belongs to the Presence within.

Come up into the mountain, rise in consciousness, and look out from that high place. All that you can see, I give unto you. I give unto you infinity, and in proportion to your receptivity do you receive. I give unto you My peace, My wholeness, the fullness of My joy, the life abundant, glorious and free.

All these I give unto you as you go higher and higher on the road to the awareness of My presence, for in My presence, consciously realized, there is fullness. You need seek no place outside yourself, but seek within your Self, for it is there that I am found because I am your Self.

The Presence is standing inside the door of our consciousness, knocking so that we will know It is there. When the first vague recognition of It as a potentiality comes, it is as if we stood in front of an awesome locked door, which is unassailable but which beckons us to sort out the key from among the burdensome accumulations we have carried around with us, which we thought of as the keys to happiness. As we fumble among them, suddenly one stands out. It is the key to the hidden mysteries. Happily, and yet not quite believing, we take it, unlock the door, fling it open, and there within us is that Presence so long sought after. Miracle of miracles, it is our Self, the *I*.